Can Leopards
Change
Their Spots?

William Jefferson

ISBN 978-1-64471-902-2 (Paperback)
ISBN 978-1-64471-903-9 (Digital)

Covenant Books, Inc.
11661 Hwy 707
Murrells Inlet, SC 29576
www.covenantbooks.com

DEDICATION

I acknowledge the reality and power of the Holy Spirit, as the cause for my release from prison and the ultimate source of my strength to endure and overcome the legal and other set-backs in my life.

I dedicate this book in love to my wonderful wife, Andrea, and to each of my daughters, their husbands and my eight, beautiful grandchildren. Thank you for your encouraging and helpful suggestions. I dedicate this book to my pastors and religious leaders in my community, many of whom have received their heavenly rewards, for their sustained prayers, spiritual teachings that empowered my commitment to God and to service to people everywhere.

Finally, I dedicate this work to David Martinez, formerly imprisoned with me at Beaumont, Texas, who introduced me to Bishop Ignatius, the main character in this book. David started me down the road of writing religious fictional novels and it has been a journey of pure joy and discovery, and I hope of enlightenment and inspiration for others.

CONTENTS

"Can the Ethiopian change his skin or the leopard his spots? Then may ye also do good that are accustomed to do evil."

—*Jeremiah 13:23 (KJV)*

PROLOGUE

CHRISTIANITY: The way it was and the way it is.

Today, Christianity has billions of adherents. Indeed, nearly one-third of the people on earth are Christians. Except for a number of heart-wrenching, well documented atrocities against small populations of Christians in Sudan, Egypt, and a few other parts of Africa, Iraq, Syria, Libya, and across the Middle East by terrorist groups, most Christians worship and practice their faith in relative peace and security. In early Christendom, however, virtually every Christian community everywhere was under siege, the assault more comprehensive near Christianity's beginnings. In the years following the crucifixion of Jesus until well into the second century, attacks on Christians were decidedly worse. As implausible as it may seem, a religion started by a man who, during His life on earth, preached, perhaps, to fewer people than would fill a professional football stadium today, and whom less than half of 1 percent of the inhabitants of the Roman Empire had ever heard of while He lived, so threatened the Empire that it killed that man and martyred thousands in an attempt to extinguish it. The vitality of Jesus's message, however, did not depend on the lives of His murdered early followers, and the messenger, Jesus, supposed by those who orchestrated His crucifixion to die with that message, proved to be not just a man, but God Incarnate, the Son of God, the Light of the World, the Word, that Fire in the bones of old prophets.

It turned out that every effort to douse that Fire spread it, like sparks leaping from one kindling to the next, setting ablaze every spiritual dry place they touched, each fire emitting more and still brighter light. This is what happened in the story told here, a story occurring in the life and through the deaths of Bishop Ignatius of Antioch, Syria and of a few of his converts. Rome's efforts to destroy Ignatius and his cause made him and it stronger. His execution gave newer and greater life to the early church, and the effects of his martyrdom ripple throughout Christian history, making him an icon of the faith.

This story demonstrates how God often uses the radical pride and vindictive rage of evil men—in this case, a fulminating Roman emperor, Trajan, who ordered an insubordinate Ignatius to be fed to the lions in the Roman Coliseum—to galvanize His movement toward the orderly establishment of His church. Were Ignatius not forced to travel as a prisoner from Syria to Rome, he would never have written seven seminal letters to churches along that way, setting out enduring Christian life lessons, church principles and practices. Were he not, during that inglorious trek, chained to ten Roman soldiers, the light of his presence would not have been showered upon them, affecting their lives and the lives of others along that awful journey. And, were it not for the misguided wrath of Trajan, Ignatius's example and his lessons about the holiness of sacrifice, even to martyrdom, would not have attracted more and more steadfast followers to Jesus and to the early church.

At its core, though, this story is about the limitless power of the Holy Spirit to tug at the hearts of even the most hardened and resistant men. It is a story of the most precious fruit of the Spirit—love—drawing men to Christ. It is also a story of God's faithfulness to exact vengeance in His Own Way and in His Own time on behalf of His own. It shows God's mysterious, yet dependable way of upsetting the evil designs of arrogant men and repositioning those designs for good. It shows how and why Christianity has become the beacon of peace and salvation of the world, as billions have received Jesus as the resurrected Son of God and accepted His immutable invitation to live in love and to gaze past the fear of death to the open heavens, depending on His promise to them to live with Him forever in unspeakable glory.

This book is a roman à clef, a novel in which some actual persons, places, and events are depicted in fictional guise. Though a work of fiction, the truths that this book calls to mind about God's love, saving power, and sovereignty, are not fictional, but are as real and as timeless as ones faith chooses to accept and receive, the prophet Jeremiah's pessimistic query notwithstanding.

CHAPTER 1

A FALSE START

"But as for you, ye thought evil against me; but God meant it unto good..."
—*Genesis 50:20 (KJV)*

Sometimes we think we know ourselves and our destinations starting out. Sometimes we believe we must remain the way we are, and stay headed in the same direction. But encounters can reveal our inner nature to us, even change us, in unexpected, even miraculous ways. And, then we may end up traveling in new, unplanned directions. Change always requires choice and acceptance by the ones affected by it. And, it always comes at a price, sometimes an exorbitant one. But, if God is in the change, it is always worth it.

Six days before the calends of March, in the 363rd year since the founding of Rome, Roman Emperor Trajan came to the city of Antioch of Syria. I met his cortege at the eastern gate of the city, accompanied by thirty-five soldiers securing his royal litter, men under my command. These men cleared the way on the front, sides, and rear of the litter, keeping the throngs that pressed to glimpse him and his parade of soldiers and dignitaries at a safe distance. Eight powerfully built, shirtless Ethiopian slaves carried his litter, balancing it so expertly that it appeared to be riding atop clouds. The tightly drawn curtains of the litter prevented the people, crane as they might, from peeking inside, where Trajan sat on a splendid purple couch in the company of two personal body guards and his longtime attaché, Crassus. I took personal charge of the security contingent as the procession entered the gate, leading to a bridge over the Orontes River. On the other side, a roadway along the river led to Emperor Trajan's Antioch palace.

Trajan's palace at Antioch was a smaller version of the ostentatious residences he occupied in Imperial Rome. Like the palaces reserved for the Emperor and his royal entourage in most major cities of the Empire, it reflected the Empire's wealth, extravagance, and stability, a vast realm at the zenith of western civilization. Indeed, Trajan's Empire covered the entire world, excepting India and lands in the Far East. So grand was the Roman Empire under Trajan that lands and peoples voluntarily submitted to his sovereignty for the coveted privilege of Roman citizenship. Those who did not so submit, if he desired, Trajan aggressively compelled with the edge of his sword. I admired him greatly as my quintessential military leader and my god. Yes, my god, as he was deified by the Roman Senate and acknowledged by the people of the empire for his many magnificent military victories and unparalleled domestic achievements in major cultural and infrastructure projects. In my eyes and in the eyes of all Rome, Trajan deserved deification. And though he was initially reluctant to claim that honor, Trajan observing, starting out, that even Julius Caesar was not deemed a god while Caesar lived, the adoration of the people and his singular accomplishments ultimately convinced him to believe himself deserving recognition and having the power and authority of a living god. My chest swelled in pride as I glimpsed him disembarking his litter for his overnight rest at his palace. "Till morning, god of Rome, Your Grace," I whispered to myself as chill bumps rose on my arms. Then, I rushed about making sure that my men were all in their proper places securing the palace.

From experience, I knew Antioch presented unique security challenges. Although, a walled city sitting on several hills, Antioch proved difficult to secure because of its openness and diversity of peoples. Apart from Greeks and Romans, Antioch contained large populations of Arabs, Africans, Asians, and Jews, each group freely bringing its own cultural offerings in architecture, song, dance, dress, literature, habits and prejudices. Race, religion, and nationality intermingle, and at times, clashed. Ironically, Antioch drew large numbers of Jews, insisting on the free exercise of their faith, while also attracting large numbers of Christians fleeing Jerusalem to escape religious persecution by the Jews of that city. Though Trajan built the walls around Antioch to protect its treasures from its enemies, the walls provided no protection from internal strife of its many friends living there. "I must leave nothing to chance," I solemnly vowed, as I determined to stay up the night fine tuning my security plans for the events Emperor Trajan had scheduled.

I went to the Antioch Palace the next morning early, at dawn's break, to acquaint the emperor's men with my plans to secure his procession and appearance at the city's amphitheater, and to get their agreement on them. But, my arrival before sunrise surprised Crassus.

"By Jupiter! You are bright and early, Captain Aurelius Maximus. The cock has not yet crowed and you are in full regalia. How far away is this place to which we must travel?" a somewhat disheveled Crassus complained.

"It isn't the distance, Your Lordship," I explained. "It is my manner to leave no detail unconsidered. Some mad men may present threats to His Excellency. I should wish that I should die and all my household before a hair should be ruffled on his head."

"Surely, you have nothing to fear in that respect," Crassus remarked, laughing, "for as you know, the emperor's hairline recedes well past his ears, and it will take quite a jostle to ruffle it. But to your point, I appreciate your dedication to Emperor Trajan." Then Crassus paused, and looking over his nose, remarked, "To be perfectly clear, though, despite that, you know that you and your household will be held to account if things do not go without a wrinkle. Yes?" His dark humor matched his rough, dark features, and his fat belly shook as that of a well-fed person with cares so few that he occupied a good part of his thoughts with ways to amuse himself. A short, stocky man, he clapped his unusually thick hands together as he laughed. His once handsome black hair was now mostly white.

"I would expect nothing less," I responded.

Crassus took a long look at me. "Your greenish eyes appear to smile beneath your thick, reddish-brown brows. The sun, just peeking out from behind his morning's thin cloud cover, appears to make your handsome, ruddy complexion radiant. Are you competing with our Emperor, adopting the look of a god?" I was stunned, speechless, as I thought he might have been serious. Then, he laughed another belly laugh. "Relax, Aurelius. I just hate morning people, people who look their best at dawn." I still hesitated, for I had early on learned to be careful not to offend Crassus. "Please, go ahead and smile, let that red mustache and beard of yours encase, that arresting smile." I stood quiet, still wary.

"With all your muscles, broad shoulders, and thick chest, all covered with that thick leather and metal breast plate filling out the trunk of your uniform, you look the part of a security commander, one whose prowess to ward off an enemy would not likely be tested, except by someone well prepared for a stiff fight. Surely you are not cowed by a fat old Roman," Crassus roared.

Now I laughed with him, as I felt the danger pass, for Crassus had a well-earned reputation as a fitful and jealous man, protective of his place and of his emperor and easily offended. "Thank you, my lord," I offered meekly, as I wanted to quickly get through the business for which I had come and to get out of his presence.

"That is why I have come as early as I have—to save the emperor's hair and my head," I wryly retorted, smiling as Crassus had ordered.

"I am forty-one years old and have devoted my entire adult life to the undivided service of Rome and Rome's emperors, especially of Emperor Trajan, even to the point that I have not as yet found space in my heart for a wife and children." I saw Crassus grow quiet now, a mild cloud of embarrassment seeming to fall over his brow, and while I had him in that state, and having claimed the higher ground from him, like a well-experienced soldier, I pounced.

"May we review the emperor's security plans for our passage to the amphitheater and for the other times he appears in public here? For the parade to the amphitheater, I suggest that we give the appearance of two royal litters, one in which the emperor will ride and one in which my security personnel will be carried. Only you, a few security soldiers, and I will know which litter bears the emperor. The curtains of each will be drawn, so no matter how much he may want to acknowledge the approving chants of the crowds, it is best if he is actually exposed to the public only when he rises to be received at the amphitheater."

A quizzical look flashed on Crassus's face. "There's a lot more to consider. This is a big city," I reassured, trying to convey a serious tone.

Indeed, Antioch had grown to over three hundred thousand people during Trajan's reign, the second largest city in the Empire.

"Of course, Aurelius," Crassus answered, brightening. "Let's retire to the palace courtyard, then, and review your plans and chat. You know how the emperor likes to be seen by his people, maybe... we'll just see. Shall we?" Then, thinking to amuse himself further, he added, "If I may say so, dear Aurelius, you appear to be as tight as a tick on one of the emperor's hounds, this morning," he chuckled. "But follow me."

Two hours later, after Crassus had approved most of my plans, while regaling me over his and Emperor Trajan's adventures and accomplishments, the emperor emerged in the palace foyer. Crassus and I leapt to our feet. Then, Crassus went over and had a private word with Trajan. I waited patiently until he beckoned me to greet Emperor Trajan.

"Emperor Caesar Nerva Trajan Augustus, Conqueror of the Germans, Conqueror of the Dacians, Conqueror of the Parthians, Son of Devine Nerva, Chief Priest, Father of the Fatherland, the Most Excellent One, the Equal of Jupiter, I, Aurelius, your humble, devoted, and grateful servant, am delighted to see you and to place myself at your complete pleasure." Then I bowed deeply and knelt before the emperor, my eyes downcast.

"Arise, arise, up, up!" Trajan ordered, impatiently dismissive of my heavy formalities. I popped up in obedience and reverence, waiting for permission to speak.

"How has the city been since my last visit? Is all well and peaceable? Have the walls been breached?" he chuckled.

A tall, big-boned man with a thick neck and athletic build, Trajan displayed a confident disposition. Dark complexioned and dignified in bearing, he had deep, penetrating eyes and high cheekbones. His bulbous nose and firm mouth gave him an overall stern appearance. Knowing Trajan detested informality, though he was indulging in a bit of it with me, I decided it best not to return it and to stick strictly to protocol.

"No, Your Excellency. The walls you built will never be breached. The city is very secure and prosperous, and under your Divine leadership, the Empire thrives. We are all well prepared for today's events, and I repeat, your Majesty, I am at your pleasure…whenever you are prepared to leave, of course. The trip should be easy and, with Mercury to guide us, take a little more than an hour."

Emperor Trajan nodded. "Oh, by the way, I will want to see the city during the procession to the amphitheater." I knew then that Crassus had briefed him on that part of the morning's security plan. "I do not want to be cloistered away from my view of the people and the surroundings—nor theirs of me. Make arrangements for that. How else can I see firsthand the outcome of the good works that we are doing?" Then, so as not to have what he'd just said taken by me as a rebuke, he continued, admiringly offering, as he turned to reenter the palace, "It is pleasant to see you again, Aurelius."

That was as close as he ever came to saying, "Thank you, Aurelius, for your good service." But I understood his meaning and bowed in gratitude.

I should have predicted Trajan's decision not to be cloistered behind curtains, for when he entered Rome to take power as emperor, he did so modestly, choosing not to ride in a gilded chariot. Romans celebrated him for instead walking into Rome on foot on that glorious day, as a man of the people, a Roman citizen like they, first and foremost.

———•———

Quite literally on the other side of town, another dignitary prepared for his trek to the Antioch Amphitheater around the same time that Aurelius and Crassus met at the palace. Kneeling in the morning darkness, in the residential quarters built by the church of Antioch of Syria for its bishop, Bishop Ignatius offered morning prayers. His austere residence bore no resemblance to Trajan's magnificent abode, nor did he desire that it do so. The third bishop of Antioch—St. Peter, the disciple of Jesus, being the first—he was one of a group of children touched and blessed by Jesus Himself, earning him the alternative name "Theophorous" (God Bearer). Trained and taught by St. John, another disciple of Jesus, brought Ignatius within the circles of men who had walked with and been taught by Jesus while He lived among them on Earth. These disciples gave firsthand accounts of His resurrection and ascension. Further, the transformation of Jesus's disciples from men so discouraged and afraid after His crucifixion that they fled back into the anonymity of their former lives, into willing martyrs for the faith, proved that they had seen Jesus alive. Thus, service in the company of Jesus's disciples and witness to their lives cemented Ignatius's certainty that Jesus was the son of God, the resurrected Messiah. Ignatius's belief, then, in the ultimate resurrection of Jesus's followers with Him, to live with Him in Paradise forever, could not be shaken.

Ignatius believed that the world as men experienced it would soon pass away. Indeed, it passed away daily. He believed that on Earth there was no lasting empire, not even that of Rome, and no lasting city, not even the stronghold, Antioch of Syria. Still daily, it seemed to him, it impeded the mission of his church to have Rome treat Christians as second-class members of society. Indeed Rome labeled Christianity an outlawed club, rather than treat it as a recognized religion. Under siege by Jewish leaders who took pleasure in harassing Christians and reporting untruthfully on their practices to Roman authorities, Ignatius stayed in constant prayer for his followers' relief. He would take the occasion of Trajan's visit to impress upon him the need to abate his people's suffering and the effect on them of Jewish leaders and others making unfounded complaints against Christ's followers to the emperor's administrators. The Christians were a peaceable people, willing to live within the laws of the land, and to bear the burdens of citizenship, he would plainly inform the emperor. Moreover, the constant frontal attacks on Christians by Jewish leaders were causing disunity, threatening to scatter them to other regions, and breeding doubt and confusion from false teachers as to what Christianity actually meant. Thus, Ignatius aimed to make

Trajan realize the harmlessness of Christian worship practices as a threat to the peace and prosperity of Rome. Perhaps, he thought, he would even be able to convince him of their value to it. By all events, he hoped that, after seeing Trajan, he would be freer to focus on the matter of building his church, rather than dealing with pointless distractions. Of course, believing Yahweh to be the one and only true God, and Jesus, His Resurrected Son, to be the Messiah, left no room for belief in the deity of Trajan. He could not fathom how, under any circumstances, a man could deify another man. However, Ignatius had no intention of challenging the deity of Trajan, as such, this morning in order to address the principal issues, he had in mind to present and discuss with him.

"Oh, God, in the name of Your Son, Jesus Christ, give me the wisdom and the courage to say what must be said for Your people this day," Ignatius prayed. "Let me be a vessel of Your sacred trust. Give me the courage to stand and speak boldly for You so men of every station may know you as God of salvation, mercy, and love. You have chosen me as Your bishop, to shepherd Your people. Make me worthy of this favored assignment. Keep me from the beguiling entreaties of this world, the deadly temptations of the flesh that destroy, the dark passages that hide your light. Keep me Your humble, contented servant, seeing no reason to live or die, save You. Now, strengthen me for this day's journey and still me in Your way. Bless Emperor Trajan for the good of the people over whom he has governance. Let him see the truth of our ministry, so that we may live tranquil lives in your service, building Your kingdom here on Earth. Reveal to him that You are the one and only true and living God. By all events let Your Divine Will be made manifest to me. And let it be done in the name of Jesus, our resurrected Savior, amen."

Arising from his praying and meditating, Ignatius opened the curtains behind his altar, receiving the glorious light and warmth of God's sunshine. He pulled his robes up and girded them. Then he went out to wash the feet of his servants, for this day, the last Friday of the month, he dedicated himself to this humbling service. Tall and gaunt, with shocks of gray hair going in every direction, a man not given to eating large meals and, at other times, given to long periods of fasting and praying, he was skinny and pale. Thus, his robes required continual readjusting. He had servants enough to attend to the proper fitting of his garments, but he preferred to take care of his own physical needs as much as possible, lending his servants and followers to attend to the needs of one another and to others in the area of their ministry. Today, though, he would travel to the amphitheater with a group from his church to bear witness to his discussion and understandings with Trajan and to assist him in navigating through the expected crowd. Although completely unexpected and certainly unplanned, what would happen this morning in his encounter with Emperor Trajan would profoundly and lastingly change him, Trajan, Crassus, Aurelius, his men, and the drawing power of the early Christian church. It would bring into sharp relief for the world to see what it ultimately meant to be a Christian.

CHAPTER 2
THE ENCOUNTER

*"I will instruct thee and teach thee in the way which
thou shalt go. I will guide thee with mine eye."*
—*Psalms 32:8 (KJV)*

By the beginning of the second century, a few years after Ignatius
became bishop of Antioch of Syria, the separation between Judaism
and Christianity in the city of Antioch was near complete. Though
some outsiders might still have been confused over that issue, the Jews
and the Christians there were not. That is the way each group wanted
it. The Jews did not desire association with a sect they deemed blas-
phemers of God and that, besides, drew constant suspicion of engag-
ing in acts of treason against the Empire. The Christians were bent on
expanding their ranks and unwilling to be bound by old practices of
Judaism, such as circumcision, observing food restrictions, Sabbath
practices, and the like. They no longer recognized the old notion
held by some earlier followers of Jesus that one had to be or become
a Jew as a predicate to becoming Christians, and likewise desired
separation from the Jews. Additionally, Christians worshiped Jesus
specifically, a deity practice of worshipping one who had walked on
the Earth as a man, something for which Judaism held no precedent.

The State of Rome had an unwitting hand in this separation,
too. Jews, as a recognized religion, paid a punitive tax to the government. Christians, as unrecognized, did not. Thus, Rome had a
self-interest in separating Jews from Christians in order to correctly
collect its taxes. The Jewish burden of taxation, however, carried with

18

it the privilege of legitimacy, primacy in access to Roman authorities, and, ultimately, a certain favor with them.

Alienated from their Jewish parents freed the Christians from seeking recruits for the Faith only from among the ranks of the Jews of Palestine, encouraging them to also forage for growth in the vast non-Jewish world of Arabia, Asia Minor, Macedonia, and the lands adjoining and across the Mediterranean Sea. Jews in these other areas felt intense pressure from these Christian competitors, both because the number of new Christian memberships was eclipsing their numbers and because Christians, zealously preaching the exciting new message of Jesus's resurrection in their synagogues, still drew members from Jewish houses of worship. This incendiary mix of Jewish and Christian angst in general, the impudence of Christians and Ignatius in particular, and the broad lack of understanding or antipathy toward Christians on the part of the Roman authorities, who considered Christians atheist for not accepting the gods of Rome, conspired to set the stage for a fiery encounter.

Leaving Trajan's Palace, I rode close to his litter. I had been unable to convince him to draw his curtains or to have two royal litters—one a decoy—in the procession. I did succeed in making an arrangement that he would draw his curtains on the left side only of his litter from and on his return to the palace. Moreover, I prevailed on my suggestion that I personally ride close on the side on which the curtains were drawn, on both the way there and back.

"You may, Aurelius. I am not sure whether to dub you a warrior or a worrier. But, so long as you and your mount stay to the rear sideedge of my litter, so as not to obstruct my view of the people or theirs of me, you may ride as you wish," Trajan conceded, good-naturedly.

The crowd teemed as we, having moved back across the Orontes River Bridge, turned onto the beautifully tiled and covered colonnade street named for Emperor Tiberius and King Herod. Trajan's large, dark eyes lit up as he reveled in the people's reverence. Trajan ordered the procession to pause for a moment to permit him to honor the Walls of Emperor Tiberius and Emperor Titus, both constructed under his administration. The crowd took the pause as an invitation to move in closer. I begged the emperor to move forward, fearing the press of the crowd might smother me and my security forces. He acquiesced reluctantly, for he enjoyed the close celebration. Visiting Antioch for the first time since pushing the Empire to its largest territorial extent, to the frontiers north and east of the Euphrates, Trajan knew that the people had heard of these victories and were giving him added high praise because of that. At his command, his barrel-chested litter carriers broke into a trot, quickly advancing the parade out of its bottleneck, leaving adoring shouts of "Hail Emperor Trajan! Hail to the God of the Empire! All hail! All hail!" in his wake.

As Trajan looked to his rear, Mount Staurin rose in the distance, standing as a natural protective boundary for Antioch. Turning his gaze forward and to the left, Mount Silpius majestically greeted us, the glow of the sun cascading over its peaks adding to its grandeur. The crowd remained large, friendly, and boisterous as the parade passed the Forum of Valens and the Theater of Caesar. The raised Antioch Aqueduct, generously improved by Trajan's administration to meet the burgeoning water and sanitation needs of the city, appeared on the horizon. A few hundred yards up, one could see the glistening waters of the reservoir that fed through the aqueduct. A half mile farther, the splendid outline of the magnificent amphitheater came into Trajan's sight. This imposing architectural wonder arose as a dividend from the internal peace of the Empire under Trajan's immediate predecessor, Emperor Nerva, Trajan's father through adoption. Under Nerva, and continuing under Trajan, the amphitheater also spoke to the flourishing cultural development of the city. Trajan had chosen it as the gathering place today to showcase Antioch's modernity and the growing sophistication and appeal of the arts in the region.

At the entrance to the amphitheater, though, stood a reminder of something far less uplifting. For all of the adulation and good feelings generated so far, this morning, the recurring, distasteful subject, the bane of many of his administrators—the ongoing internecine conflict between Christians and Jews—confronted Trajan. On the right side of the amphitheater's entrance stood a very large crowd of Jews. Trajan could not see them because his curtains were drawn on that side, but they were perfectly visible to me from the back of my steed. I recognized them at once, and their high priest, Jonas. I had informed the emperor and Crassus that the amphitheater was situated near a very large and vibrant Jewish community—indeed, just south of it—and that many Jews would be there to pay homage to him and to thank him for assisting them with a vital project. The emperor was pleased to hear that. Yet, neither he nor I had anticipated the presence of a smaller, but still a goodly sized, ragtag band facing off against the Jews on the other side of the entrance.

"Christians," I muttered to myself.

I had run across Ignatius in conducting my responsibilities to secure the city. I had not spoken to him, though I had heard him speak passionately about his faith. I'd found it somewhat amusing, excited as he was over an apparent mystical belief in what seemed to me a discussion about, at best, a ghost. I had been instructed to tolerate him and his fellow Christians so long as they kept the peace and did not appear fanatical. I had concluded that these so-called Christians gathered for the exercise of a harmless superstition, rather than for the treachery of treason. However, I noticed standing close to him this morning two of his associates, Zachariah and Gabriel, whom I had had occasion in the past to question about their organizing work among the poor, on reports that they were talking of violence. In that instance I had found them harmless and the anonymous accusations unsupportable.

Unfortunately for Ignatius and his followers this morning, standing on the left side of the entrance to the amphitheater, gave Trajan a full view of their miserable and dour appearance. The look of shock and disgust registered on Trajan's face conveyed that he immediately took offense to their presence. I doubted that this was because they looked poor and unkempt, for there were many in the crush of that appearance.

I guessed that this group of dregs viscerally repulsed Trajan because they were not cheering him like the others in the crowd, not acclaiming him, not appearing to acknowledge him in any way. Some of my men later told me that, during the hour or so it took him to travel from his palace to the amphitheater, the Jews had jeered and insulted Ignatius and his followers, berating them for nearly all that time, demanding that they leave their community. But, neither Emperor Trajan nor I had any idea why this Christian band appeared in such a foul, uncheerful mood.

"Who are those people?" Crassus shouted in my direction, referring to Ignatius's pack we had just passed. A deep frown creased his face.

"Christians," I replied cryptically.

As Trajan's entourage came to a halt just inside the amphitheater, an ear-splitting, sustained roar, accompanied by chants of exultation for Trajan erupted on the right side of his litter, compelling Trajan's attention. "*Jews,*" I thought.

"Who are those people?" a marveling Crassus asked, with Trajan suddenly seeming interested in the answer to that question.

"Jews, my Lord," I responded. "A very large assemblage of Jews!" I continued enthusiastically.

"These are the ones here to thank Emperor Trajan?"

I nodded agreement.

"If it pleases you, Emperor Trajan, could I have Aurelius see that their leaders are brought to the palace when your events are concluded?" Crassus inquired excitedly.

Emperor Trajan waved an accommodating, unenthusiastic, yes.

Then, Crassus directed me. "See that the leaders of the Jewish group are later brought to the palace."

"Of the Jews?" I inquired.

"Yes," Crassus said.

Then, he paused.

"And of the Christians too!" Crassus added, looking to Trajan for approval.

Trajan added, "By all means, yes. I need to hear from these atheists."

I went to Jonas.

"The emperor invites you and a small group of your people to meet him at the palace at the conclusion of today's program," I reported to him, to which he gleefully and gratefully responded. "Oh, please thank the emperor. We would be more than honored."

I then called on Ignatius.

"The emperor requires your presence at the palace when this event ends," I said matter-of-factly.

Confusion registered on the faces of Ignatius and his group.

"To what end I do not know," I said, intentionally leaving them in the torment of their worst thoughts.

"Just two or three of you," I said, adding to the suspense.

The invitation to visit Trajan at his palace was more than Ignatius had hoped for, on the one hand. He'd not really figured out the details of how the opportunity to address Trajan about his issues would develop. He had trusted that God would provide a way. He had prayed for the words to say, feeling confident that God would use him to speak for Him when the time and place to speak arose. On the other hand, the way this meeting came about made him wary. In his spirit, he felt trouble afoot.

He had not been offered an invitation he could refuse. Captain Aurelius had told him that his presence at the palace was required, not desired. The added measure of the emperor assigning security to him to make sure that he kept his appointment at the palace seemed a bad omen.

———•———

"Disgusting," I heard Ignatius comment, as he walked into the palace. He looked over the extravagance—the rich marble floors and walls, the gilded draperies and furnishings, the beautiful fountains flowing with water and wine, the glistening white columns, the elaborately dressed courtiers and servants, the beautiful works by world-class artists and sculptors, and the gleaming columns reaching for the sky.

"Every day, I work with the poorest of the poor in this city," Ignatius said, loudly enough for me and several of my men to hear.

"And," he continued, "this waste is painful, intolerable, boastful of self-importance. This palace is maddening."

As we passed the images of the gods of Rome, Ignatius became more agitated. "Lord," he said softly, "forgive me for my presence in the midst of the idolatry of these claimed gods of the Roman Empire, the lesser gods of his household, and the altar to Trajan himself."

"Shut up, old fool" I muttered at Ignatius. "Another disrespectful word and I will end your miserable life before you see Emperor Trajan!"

Ignatius stared at me, as if willing to confront me further, but his men took his arm and led him forward.

I took personal offense to Ignatius's failure to bow to Trajan's altar and those of the gods of Rome. My guards and I whispered among ourselves at Ignatius's arrogance. Ignatius and his men walked past our gods as if they meant nothing, both when they entered the palace and observed these images at its doorway and upon entering the outer court leading to the inner court where Emperor Trajan sat. From the disdain on the faces of the emperor's guards and soldiers, I could tell that they felt, as we did—Ignatius's snub amounted to an act of anarchy.

My men directed Ignatius and his two companions to an ante-room, instructing them to wait quietly there while the Jewish leaders met with Trajan ahead of them. We left the door to the ante-room open so that, Ignatius and his men could hear laughter wafting from the court where Trajan, Jonas, and his people met.

Nothing good for us can come out of that laughter, Ignatius thought. *Lord, help me to discern how best to serve you today.*

• ———— • ———— •

I went into the place where the Jewish leaders met with Trajan, at the invitation of Crassus, for he beckoned me in urgently seeming amused. I do not know what went on before I entered the inner court, but Crassus gleefully dove into questioning Jonas.

"Tell me again, Jonas, in the presence of Aurelius, whose job it is to secure Antioch, are these Christians we saw today for us or against us?"

Appearing a little confused, Jonas replied," As I said earlier my Lord, they are against us, my Lord. Decidedly so. They are against Rome and against us, as supporters of the Emperor. They engage in lewd, shocking practices, even human sacrifices and live among catacombs—tombs, I mean, among the dead. And…"

"And have you told Captain Aurelius about the threat they present to Antioch, to Rome?"

"Oh, yes, my Lord. Captain Aurelius is well aware of our concerns about the dangers they present to good order and decency."

"And what has Captain Aurelius done to rid Antioch of this threat? Why were they permitted to be in our parade, close enough to strike our emperor?"

"All right, Crassus, you've had your fun, now you want to implicate Aurelius in some sort of malfeasance. I won't have that," Trajan light-heartedly broke in.

Then, Trajan turned serious.

"Surely you exaggerate, Jonas," Trajan said sternly. "I've had Christians investigated throughout my realm by many dependable administrators. They have told me that these Christians, or whatever they call themselves, assemble suspiciously at night, well, in any case before daylight, and recite a form of words to Christ as some sort of superstitious god; that they bind themselves by oath, not for any crime, but not to commit theft, or robbery or adultery; not to break their word and not to deny a deposit. After these daybreak meetings, I am told that it is their custom to depart—and to take ordinary food. I discovered nothing but an extravagant superstition. Many of them, when confronted with execution for the mere fact of claiming to be Christians, I have instructed my administrators to give them a second and third chance to repent, or at least to make supplication with wine and incense at my statute, which most do. Those who do not may face execution, but I make no general rule against the presence of Christians in Rome. I do not have them sought out and punished; however, if they are accused, not anonymously mind you, but forthrightly of committing crimes against our gods without repentance, then punishment is demanded."

Then Trajan paused, a twinkle in his eyes.

"Besides, Jonas, it may be smart on my part and yours, since there is a growing multitude of these Christians, to provide a pathway to reclaim them for Rome by creating a place for their repentance."

"Your Excellency shows such grace and kindness, but I—we have lived with them much longer than any of your administrators possibly could, and I must say to you, that they are a treacherous lot. But, you will see for yourself, and soon. This Ignatius who you will soon encounter—he will not bow to your image or make libations at the feet of your statue. He is bent on changing—destroying our way of life. He, their leader, is a very dangerous man."

Crassus looked somber at those words. Trajan drew grim. He ordered me to leave the room as he questioned Jonas and his men further.

A half hour later, Crassus sent a palace guard to the anteroom door, announcing that the time had come for Ignatius and his party to meet with Trajan.

"His Excellency summons you now. Make haste and consider yourself among the most fortunate of men on Earth to be permitted into his court," I said.

At about that time, I saw Jonas and his crew, dressed fit to see a king, brimming with happiness, pass Ignatius's shabby lot. I then said in my heart, "these two groups are going in two very different directions." The smirk on Jonas's face as he glanced at Ignatius announced an unmistakable feeling of advantage.

Trajan, sitting on a raised throne with all of the emblems of the Empire emblazoned on it, coldly received Ignatius and his men.

"Bring them forth," Trajan announced when he saw Ignatius at the entrance of his court.

Ignatius tightened his robes and distributed his clothing in as proper a fashion as he could.

Without greeting Ignatius, the emperor launched into biting questions.

"You are Bishop Ignatius, of which I have heard, are you? Bishop of what?"

"Your Excellency, Emperor Trajan, I am Ignatius, also known as Theophorus, for I bear Christ in my breast. I am bishop of the church of Antioch of Syria, appointed in an unbroken succession, succeeding Bishop Evodius, who was appointed by our beloved St. Peter, who was appointed by Jesus Christ Himself. These men, Zachariah and Gabriel, are deacons of our church. Thank you for this audience. There are certain matters I would like to discuss…"

"What brought you to my parade today?"

"I came in the hope to speak with you for…"

"It appeared to me and to my people that you came to create a disturbance."

"Oh no, Your Excellency. That is not our way, the Christian way."

"What does a bishop do?"

"He loves and guides his people, and the leaders of the church as well, into the truths and habits of Christian life. He cares for the flock entrusted to him by Jesus Christ, our resurrected Savior."

"Is this Jesus of whom you speak the same Jesus crucified under Pontius Pilate?"

"The very same, and the same who conquered death that He might establish His kingdom here on Earth. Jesus is risen and alive, and lives in each one who believes in Him. His Kingdom is within each of us."

"Do you bear Christ in you"?

"Most certainly. For it is written, 'I will dwell in and walk among My people.'"

"How many of you Jesus Followers are there in Antioch, in my Empire?" Trajan asked in a loud voice, evincing a bit of exasperation, Ignatius's confident responses and the fact that Ignatius appeared not to be awed in his presence clearly irritating him.

"There are many and many more to come, through the grace of God. An exact number I know not."

"You will give no more slippery responses. You will answer the emperor's questions directly, completely, and respectfully. No more preposterous exchanges! Most importantly, you will not further this absurd dialogue about a risen Jesus living in you. Whom do you really serve? What purpose does your club serve? Are you prepared to bend your knees to the power of Imperial Rome, represented in the person of our Emperor Trajan?" Crassus thundered.

Instead of crushing Ignatius, Crassus's attack seemed to delight him, looking as if a light went off inside of him, as if he welcomed the chance to explain his god and his faith directly to Trajan. His answer to Crassus was calm and resolute.

"I am not wise enough to respond to you on my own account, in my own power. I live and I breathe only for the sake of Jesus Christ. His Holy Spirit directs my path and my lips. Through His grace, I can only speak the truth of His reality. We also want to serve Him in peace. We want to give due honor to the Roman Empire and to Emperor Trajan."

"Do you believe in the immortal gods of Rome, who assist and protect us against our enemies?" Crassus pounded away, cutting directly to the issue at hand, to get to the heart of disloyalty to Rome, if there be any.

Ignatius now realized his inescapable position. Could this be an orchestrated confrontation? He could not be sure that the pointed questions being put to him had not been suggested to Trajan and Crassus by the visitors to the palace who had immediately preceded him. This was not the meeting he had so carefully prepared for at his early-morning rising. He resigned himself, whatever the origin of or cause for the question, to remain true to his faith and his God.

"There is but one God, who made the heavens, earth, and seas and all that is within them, and one Christ Jesus, His only begotten, whose friendship I enjoy."

"Atheist! Incorrigible Atheist! Imposter! Then what is Emperor Trajan, if not a god, worthy of worship, worthy of your honor and reverence? Is Emperor Trajan a god in your heart and mind or is he not?"

Ignatius swallowed hard. Then he straightened his back. He took a moment to look upward. Then, he looked Trajan directly in the eye.

"I know only one God, and one Son and one Holy Spirit. I respect and honor Emperor Trajan as my emperor, but not as my god. The kingdom of God of which I speak is not of this earth and is not in opposition to any earthly government, and certainly not in opposition to the Roman Empire. It is only in opposition to sin. Our work is not to change earthly kingdoms but to change the hearts of men. The kingdom within us is a kingdom of love for one another and peace on earth. It is a kingdom of God, not of men. That is the mystery of our faith," Ignatius responded in a soft, serene voice.

Crassus seemed moved by Ignatius's statement, for he sat back from the edge of his seat in contemplation. He observed Ignatius carefully. Trajan himself seemed confounded, as Crassus, after a long pause, whispered something in his ear.

Ignatius mystified me. As a soldier, I had often envisioned circumstances where, captured by an enemy, I might face certain death. Would I be able to die gracefully, bravely facing it down? I had always concluded that I could, but I had never actually been put to that specific test. I felt that Bishop Ignatius stood in that place tonight, soon to be in a battle for his life, were he not already. Yet strangely, he did not appear to be concerned with that, giving reckless answers. A mix of a bit of sorrow, grudging respect, and an ardent curiosity about him momentarily engulfed me, taking over a part of me. However, the other part of me, the larger part, was inflamed by his stiff, unflinching demeanor—his uncalled-for hardheadedness. Trajan was emperor, after all, and a god after all, undeniably so! Standing before him demanded more than civility. It required resolute worship. That was the way of our world! What prevented Ignatius from seeing and complying with this simple reality? Were he wise enough to lead a sect of large and devoted members, why not wise enough to see what he must do to save himself and his club?"

Crassus began, again, speaking more slowly, even with a measure of warmth.

"It appears that you may have unintentionally insulted the emperor. Unintentionally, you may have questioned his deity. If it be proven otherwise, well, no man lives who does that! By his grace, however, Emperor Trajan has agreed to give you the chance to clear this matter and to save your life. A cult, like yours, that encourages love and peace may have its usefulness. Yet no god can be placed above our immortal gods, and Emperor Trajan is their equal. If you choose to engage in the superstition of Jesus Christ, then that foolishness may be indulged," he sneered, laughing, "but you cannot honor Him above our immortals nor can you deny the deity of Trajan. If you renounce Jesus Christ as a god not superior to Jupiter, and not superior to our other immortal gods nor to Emperor Trajan, the emperor may spare your life and you may continue working within and leading your cult. If not, then, by the order of Emperor Trajan, which order is not subject to reversal by the hand of man or god, you shall surely be condemned to die."

Ignatius looked upon Trajan and Crassus with sorrow and pity.

"I can only speak the truth as I know it and as the Holy Spirit prompts me. I feel consumed now by the Holy spirit and can only say to you that which He gives to me. Here are His words, not mine":

"Let no one be deceived. Even heavenly beings and the angels in their glory, and rulers visible and invisible—even for these there will be judgment, if they do not believe in the blood of Christ."

"What do you mean by this foolish drivel? Do you take my warnings for a trifle? Speak plainly so that it may be unmistakable that you have sentenced yourself to death. Answer me directly. This is your last chance!" Crassus yelled, now completely red-faced.

The indignation of Ignatius rose up in him. That a man should think himself above Christ was dangerous folly! Yet he prayed for a quiet spirit that he would not respond in anger but in humility.

"My life is a small matter compared to my hope for eternal life in paradise with Jesus. The Father raised Him from the dead, and in the same manner He shall raise me up in Christ Jesus. This is what I believe. This is all that I believe."

Trajan could no longer hold his anger.

"Are you mad?" Trajan scowled. "Then raise you up He must. For I, on this day, sentence you to death by the teeth of the beasts in the Imperial City of Rome, home of the gods you have spurned. I shall be present to witness the lions tearing you limb from limb after disemboweling you. This is your just desert for blasphemy of our gods and for disobeying my direct order through Crassus, who speaks with my voice, and from me as well, to renounce Jesus. Further, I suspect, because of your mercurial responses to my inquiries, despite your protests otherwise, that you and your cult are engaged in activities that threaten the stability of the realm. Perhaps when your sorry band of followers—of Jesus Followers—also witness your demise, the "many, many" numbers of them of which you boast may be reduced to a size small enough to be more easily accounted for, since you say you cannot presently count them."

Ignatius looked up toward heaven and said with a loud voice, "What fools! Thank you, Lord. Let Your will be done. Make me worthy, without wavering, for this awesome work to which You have assigned me this day. Forgive them. I pray that they may come into the knowledge of You and repent of their sins!" Then he closed his eyes, his lips moving in silent prayers of praise and thanksgiving.

Zachariah and Gabriel dissembled into tears. They hugged Ignatius, expressing love for him, pledging to carry on his work, asking him how they should resist this unrighteous order of death.

"We will gladly suffer death with you," they both pledged.

"No," Ignatius said in a whisper. "This is my cross to bear. Our work continues through God and you as His tools until He should send Antioch another bishop. This is all for His glory. Do not be afraid for me. Tell the brethren that I go willingly to die for the cause of Christ, to lift Him up so that men may be drawn to Him."

"Break up this conspiracy," Crassus ordered.

"What of these scoundrels, Your Excellency?" Crassus asked, referring to Zachariah and Gabriel. "They have stood with him without protesting his insolence!"

"Let them be. Let them bear witness to the others of their cult of the fate of their fallen leader. They mean nothing to me. Leave them to wander headless!"

Ignatius nodded for them to leave quickly, thanking them for their love and loyalty.

The palace was quiet for a few minutes as Crassus and Emperor Trajan conferred at some length. Then Trajan spoke to me. "Aurelius," Trajan called to me, "I am assigning you to see that this criminal makes it to Rome—to my coliseum there—to his death. This bishop of Antioch has already told me of his large number of adherents. I want to make certain that none of them are successful in freeing him, of aiding his escape. If that happens, we may have another story of a resurrection on our hands. He will probably say that our soldiers killed him on the way to Rome and that he's come back from the dead, like his Jesus," he laughed, with Crassus, and others in the court. My men, and I heartily joined in.

"By Mercury, Aurelius," Trajan continued, "travel well for me to Rome with this...this...bishop, to carry out my sentence. Take ten men with you, no fewer than that, more if you deem necessary, and chain them to Ignatius day and night until he is fed to my lions. Parade him before his Christian churches and households along the way. Exhibit him in the public squares. Spare no abuse of him if he resists your orders in any way, so long as he still breathes when you get him to Rome. Bring under your gladius and spear any man who opposes your treatment of him, or who makes public objection that he is your prisoner. I trust only your command of this troop. I trust you to deliver him to Rome. By his conduct before me in my court and in my processional, he has made a mockery of me, our gods, and the Roman Empire. He will not mock us further by avoiding my sentence. Let him be mocked all the way to Rome. Let him be mocked as he meets his just fate in the arena of our beasts!

"Get him out of my sight!"

At this, Ignatius shouted, "Repent! Repent! In the name of Jesus Christ, repent and live. Only Jesus is Lord."

I grabbed Ignatius, feeling his bony body in my hands, and slammed him to the courtyard floor. He winced in pain and shock.

"Silence!" I commanded him. "Bring the chains!" I yelled. "Fasten them tight."

In my zeal, I thought, *I feel sorry for the lions. As emaciated as he is, he won't make much of a meal for them.* I smiled broadly, proud of my clever thought and of this work with which my beloved emperor honored me, my emperor who looked on approvingly at my rough handling of this Ignatius.

Overwhelmed by Emperor Trajan's confidence, I went to my quarters and I prayed. "Oh, Jupiter, Greatest and Best, I beseech and entreat thee to cause, in facility and safety, a victory in this journey to Rome for the benefit of my emperor, Caesar, son of the deified Nerva, Nerva Trajan Augustus Germanicus, our prince and our parent, chief priest, father of the Fatherland, and to him give a goodly outcome of all of those matters which now he is executing, and in particular in this matter of the just punishment of Ignatius and all of his ilk, who would dishonor you and my emperor. Bring me and my troops to Rome in the earliest possible time, and restore us to Syria and Antioch in due time. And, if you so do this, I vow in the name of College of the Arval Brethren that you shall have a gilded ox."

Chapter 3
To Rome with Love

"Come with me from Lebanon, my spouse, with me from Lebanon: Look from the top of Amana, from the top of Shenir and Hermon, from the lion's dens, from the mountains of the leopards.
—The Song of Solomon 4:8 (KJV)

A sorrier sight of a man I had not seen, even among enemy prisoners I had captured from some of the world's most god-forsaken outposts. When transporting a prisoner and food was scarce, I always saw to feeding my soldiers first, so as to enable them to carry out their mission. If a prisoner starved, he starved. As the emperor's special detail to transport this unique prisoner from Antioch to Rome, for us food and drink were plentiful and excellent. Since Trajan had sentenced Ignatius to die, he had been under my watch for several weeks. I offered Ignatius the same meals that my men ate, for there was no shortage. But even were there, I was not permitted to let him die in our hands. I struggled getting him to eat enough to satisfy me that he was healthy enough to complete this trip to Rome. Ignatius insisted on fasting and praying, eating sparingly. He assured me that he had no interest in starving to death before we made it to Rome.

"Fasting with praying is my present sacrifice of suffering to Jesus, to find greater nearness to Him in this moment. I have lived well more than eighty years, a goodly part of that time fasting for the cause of Christ. Far from a path of escape from the beasts of the Coliseum, fasting and praying are to perfect me that I may be worthy of suffering death there in His name," Ignatius quietly declared to me. "God will give me the strength I need for the trip, His trip."

Though, on the outside, he looked frail and weak, he stood as erect as a statue, and I perceived a certain inward strength and resilience in my early dealings with him. He refused the fine togas and tunics supplied him by his deacons and friends, insisting on wearing the clothing of the lowest rank, of a slave or a prisoner. I was somewhat embarrassed by the thought that, looking upon him, others might wonder why such an apparent vagabond commanded the splendid escort we provided.

I chose ten fit, seasoned, and honorable soldiers to secure Ignatius's delivery to Rome for execution. To a man, they bore the scars of battles well fought and won. These they wore as perpetual marks of military courage and pride. Their scars showed in the most visible places—their arms, legs, ankles, necks, and faces, so that any who so much as glanced at any of them quaked with fear. Together, the ten and I had amassed forty-six ceremonial medals, coins, and battle prizes. Among other decorations, Marius and Publius wore the mural crown, a military award given a soldier first to gain the wall of an enemy fortress; Antonius and Dentatus, ceremonial spears awarded for expertise in lunging the spear and the javelin in combat; heavy bracelets and necklaces adorned the wrists and necks of each soldier, including Ruffinus, Decimus, Otho, and Quintas, obvious decorations for valor; and Minucius, Valerius, and I had fastened to our uniforms several civic crowns of oak leaves each, for saving the life of a fellow soldier in battle.

I outfitted each man with leg and body armor, including bronze shin guards and metal and leather breastplates. Each carried a dagger, a gladius, a shield, and other appropriate offensive and defensive weapons. The shields were the kind usually reserved for use by centurions, with the imposing marks and insignia of Emperor Trajan. Their bright red and rust tunics, with gold embroidery, set the ten apart as members of a royal regiment. Their leather and bronze helmets were decorated with ostrich plumes of purple, orange, and red, which they sometimes were allowed to switch out, due to the heat, and replace with silver and gold gilded and clustered wreaths, made of attractive seasonal leaves and branches. My uniform was red and gold with a cape and a centurion's headdress. The vine-staff, a centurion's symbol of supreme authority and command, placed in my hands by Emperor Trajan himself, announced in whose name we served our present mission. With these escorts for Ignatius's funeral march to Rome, I felt confident that it would take nearly a company of ordinary soldiers to extract him from our grasp. Certainly, no band of nonmilitary citizens could do that, including no party of fanatical Christians or Christian sympathizers. We were well-trained and determined to make examples of anyone who might muster the courage to try us.

We set out on our journey to Rome on the first day of the second week of April, assembling at Trajan's palace, where Ignatius had been held for the several weeks since his arrest. Destined for our first stop at the Antioch church, Ignatius's headquarters, we were on keen alert for trouble. Naturally, word had spread far and wide of Ignatius's condemnation. We intended to make Ignatius a gross example of the price to be paid by anyone, especially any Christian, guilty of contemptuous or seditious conduct before our emperor, this day and every day of our trip. Dragging him in chains through the streets of Antioch and then, later, before an assembly of his churchmen seemed the perfect place to start humiliating him. Surprisingly, as it turned out, Ignatius had in mind that we should make his church our first stop, too, but for a very different reason.

"I beg you, as a citizen of Rome, that I be paid the common courtesy of bidding farewell to my beloved family at the Antioch church who will see me on these shores no more."

He requested a courtesy usually extended to a condemned person—a final visit from his family. The church members, his only family, could not be brought to the palace to pay respects. We mutually agreed that he would be taken to visit with his followers and friends at his church. He also asked another thing.

"I should like to write to churches under my authority, and some church leaders, to offer them guidance and instruction."

Crassus thought granting this permission would be useful for the government's purposes. Since I or one of my men would be used to deliver the letters, either to the churches themselves or to those ferrying them to these churches, we could, of course, read them first for any threats or crimes they might be designed to foment. Ignatius's desires to meet with his followers in place after place—starting with Antioch—and to write to them fit well with our plans to embarrass and harass him along the way in front of his Jesus Followers, as well as to better identify the members of his cult and its leaders for surveillance. To this end we agreed to permit church leaders to visit with him along the way to Rome. He also requested that his secretary, Jonathan, be permitted to visit and travel with him, to take down some of the letters or notes he dictated. I granted this request also.

I made Ignatius walk the several miles to the Antioch church. Surprisingly, he walked with strength and a show of pride. I set him a pace or two ahead of my chariot, which was drawn by two muscular, white Arabian horses. The horses snorted hot breath, and their open mouths occasionally dripped saliva on Ignatius's robe, to the amusement of my men. He seemed more frightened of these huge animals on his heels than, he claimed, of the lions in Rome. Dentatus walked slightly ahead of Ignatius, holding fast to his shield and the chains that bound Ignatius to him. Thin chains were fastened to Ignatius's hands, waist, and feet. Though he'd been given enough space between his ankles to stride freely as he walked, the ankle bracelets to which his chains attached were clamped, purposely, painfully tight. We supplied a wagon pulled by other horses to carry supplies and to spell Ignatius from walking as I saw the need to do so. Each of my men rode an impressive mount, though one walked alongside him today, his gladius in hand, to further intimidate the anticipated crowds.

This morning, for nearly two hours Ignatius walked, jerked along by chains attached to all ten men, in a dominating and brutal show of force and superiority on our part and subjugation on his. Jonas and a large group of his followers cheered us on, verbally castigating Ignatius, as did many others, but every long or tear-stained face in the crowd we identified as that of a Christian. There were not many of them. I was not sure whether that meant a paucity of Christians or that they hid themselves. We preferred the latter, for that would mean they feared us.

They were a mysterious bunch, these Christians, meeting secretly in each other's homes and even in underground cemeteries, called catacombs, with tunnels and graves. We believed these dark practices were meant to instill fear in us Romans. Today we were turning the tables.

As we entered the yard of the church, the crowd gasped loudly in obvious shock. Ignatius's ankles, already red and sore, appeared to betray him as he stumbled in the grass of the lawn. Sweat covered him from the heat of the near-midday sun, and his thin prisoner's garb stuck to his skin, exposing even more his bony frame. As we brought our march to a halt, Publius pulled Ignatius's chain, literally, tripping him into an awkward fall. We broke into roaring laughter.

"Rise up! Rise up, Bishop Ignatius!" Publius mocked. "Didn't you say that your Jesus would raise you up? Well, now is a good time for Him to do it, don't you think?" And we laughed some more.

But then several of the men in the crowd, led by Gabriel and Zachariah, who had accompanied Ignatius to Trajan's palace, charged forward to assist him. My men raised their gladii. A few of the men held back then, but Gabriel and Zachariah and a handful of others kept coming forward, until they reached Ignatius. I prevented my men from running them through. Ignatius scrambled to his feet, pushing away Gabriel and the rest, insisting on standing under his own strength, adjusting his robes as he seemed always to be doing, and shouting, "Let them be! Let them be! Do what you will with me, but leave them alone. Must you kill the deacons of God's church, too, to make your point?" Then, to the crowd he said, "I am fine. I will be fine. Please, Gabriel, please, Zachariah, hold back. There is enough evil underway this morning already."

Gabriel and the rest retreated.

"Please," he said, turning to us, "let me enter the sanctuary to pray and for Sunday Eucharist."

We entered the small, unpretentious, unsanctioned church building—a modest one-story main structure with other small buildings attached, including the simple residence that had been home to Ignatius. The church looked like an unusually built and appointed large residence. Ignatius waved the audience to either side as we guardedly made our way toward the front. The crowd swelled inside as those without the church building pressed in. I signaled to my men to take defensive positions. But, no sign of aggression toward us appeared. Only tears and wails of mourning accompanied our way.

I had previously questioned Ignatius about his request to conduct a Communion service at the Antioch church, a service, the breaking of bread, the figurative eating of the body of Christ, that he explained was the highest act of Christian worship. I had permitted it only when he swore it involved no human sacrifice and no depraved worship among the catacombs.

Ignatius admonished those carrying on as mourners, urging them to begin the celebration of the Communion, undertaking it with the usual joy, in spite of the cruelness of his circumstances. As if in an instant, their tears arrested, and the erstwhile lake of mourners became an ocean of lovers, moving into one another's arms, kissing cheeks, and openly expressing affection. Seeing no harm, and inquisitive, besides, I allowed many to kiss the bound hands of Ignatius as well, in what he called the "Kiss of Peace." After this lengthy exhibition, broken pieces of bread were passed out, and Zachariah read from a papyrus codex:

"The Lord Jesus, on that same night in which He was betrayed, took the bread; and when He had given thanks, He broke it and said, 'Take, eat; this is My body, which is broken for you; do this in remembrance of Me.' In the same manner, He took the cup after supper, saying, 'This cup is the new covenant of My blood. This do, as often as you drink it, in remembrance of Me. For as often as you do eat this bread and drink this cup, you proclaim the Lord's death until He comes again.'"

Common cups of wine were passed through the crowd, from which each congregant slightly tasted.

Ignatius then spoke again, appearing to have gained renewed strength, as he loudly cried out:

"Oh, God, hear our prayer."

Then, he urged the assemblage, "Let's pray for our church, the people of Syria, our emperor and these men." And then each person in the large crowd, to a man and woman, with bowed head, joined their voices, praying for their church, their neighbors, and then for our souls, for our families, and for our repentance—even for Trajan. We shouted at them to stop praying for us, but they would not do so. We could do nothing but listen to them in amazement, for none of us felt any cause to strike them. For the next fifteen minutes or so, with different ones of them leading the prayers, they prayed to a fever pitch for us, for Rome, for the Antioch church, and for Jesus Followers everywhere, none more than Ignatius, until Ignatius cried, "amen" in a loud voice, whereupon the praying ceased.

What manner of people are these? I thought. And observing the odd looks on the faces of my men, I don't believe I was the only one with that question in mind.

Under Ignatius's further direction, Gabriel read from a second area of the codex:

"Though I speak with the tongues of men and of angels, but have not love, I have become sounding brass or a clanging cymbal. And, though I have the gift of prophecy, and understand all mysteries and all knowledge, and though I have faith, so that I could remove mountains, but have not love, I am nothing. And, though I bestow all my goods to feed the poor and though I give my body to be burned, but have not love, it profits me nothing.

"Love suffers long and is kind; love does not envy; love does not parade itself, is not puffed up; does not behave rudely, does not seek its own, is not provoked, thinks no evil; does not rejoice in iniquity, but rejoices in the truth; bears all things, believes all things, hopes all things. Love never fails."

Finally, Ignatius addressed the assembly.

"This is my farewell to you, my beloved church. I go to be with Christ. This is the hope for each of us and, one day, in God's time, you will rest in His bosom in heaven and live with Him, the prophets, and me. Give no thought to my earthly welfare. I am in the hands of God, soon to be in His presence. God Himself must be your bishop until He gives you a new Earthly one to continue building the kingdom of Jesus Christ. When your new bishop comes, obey him, follow him, as he follows Christ. Respect and follow the deacons whom I leave with you, as well as the presbyters, as the council of God and College of the Apostles."

"Stay unified in body and spirit. Do not become ensnared in false doctrines. Teach and grow in the certainty of your belief in the passion and resurrection of Christ. Through God's Holy Spirit, love each other passionately, as Christ has loved you. And, just as powerfully, love your enemies as Jesus taught. Break the bread of the Eucharist together, the antidote to death in this world, the medicine of immortality in the next."

"God, the Father, will keep you. Jesus Christ will intercede for you and the Holy Spirit will comfort you. Though bound, I go freely to Rome. May God bring these men and any in this world who oppose the truth of Jesus into the knowledge of Him."

Zachariah pushed a papyrus into Ignatius's hands. "Your favorite Scripture," I heard him say. "Please, you read this one." And so he did.

"For I am persuaded that neither death nor life, nor angels nor principalities nor powers, nor things present nor things to come, nor height nor depth, nor any other created thing shall be able to separate me from the love of God which is Christ Jesus our Lord." Ignatius looked over his friends and followers for the final time, and with bells of joy ringing in his voice, said simply, "And so may it always be with you as well." Then, he looked toward me. "Thank you," he said. "Now, I am ready to go."

"Oh," he said, as a fastidious afterthought, showing no effects of his grim circumstances, "remember the 'fragmentum' to preserve unity. Share a piece of the bread from this communion with other churches in the city." Then, he nodded to us to leave.

Muted cries and silent tears fell heavily behind us as we took Ignatius away. Seeing this, he stopped, again urging them not to mourn for him. "Celebrate the rest of the day's Communion service, continuing to feast together and celebrate the commencement of my newly begun phase of service to God," he said as a final word.

As we made the long way to the fort outside of Antioch, where we would spend the next several days, I pondered the words and deeds of that assembly and, mostly, Ignatius's puzzling words. I didn't understand them. But, strangely, I wanted to.

We stayed at the barracks at the fort for several days, organizing and planning our trip. Ignatius's fellow Christians, some leaders of his cult from other cities, besieged us with requests to visit him, speaking of him as if he were a god. Many petitions came from them, begging us to release and restore him. Requests also came to us from churches that Ignatius be allowed to visit the cities of their location on his road to Rome. We had several choices of a route to take that would get us to Rome. One took us by the heavily populated seacoast routes and the other more inland. Either way, at the end of the day, we'd have to go by sea to the peninsula of Italy and thence overland to the imperial city itself and its coliseum—site of horrors for Ignatius and of entertainment for the civilized world. All of these became points of decision we based on the dictates of security.

We could not avoid passing through Tarsus on our route to Rome. We decided against taking a sea route there, though, because pirates operated along its coast, making our troop possible targets for a well-contrived sea attack, perhaps giving the attackers cover as random outlaws, when they might have been organized efforts by Christians to pluck Ignatius from the grasp of death.

Moreover, that St. Paul, a patron of the Christian church, beheaded in Rome, was born in Tarsus heightened our concerns for security. Would Christian fanatics, obsessed with their own martyrdom, charge us in Tarsus? Would Christians, not caring about their own lives, attempt to do a glorious work for their Jesus by rescuing his high-ranking representative, Ignatius? Thus, we traveled overland to Tarsus, located on an important military and commercial route between Rome and Syria on the northeastern shore of the Mediterranean Sea. Though concerned for the length of the trip toward Tarsus, as we started out, we moved swiftly. After a week, we glimpsed Lake Rhegma, near the sea and just a short distance from Tarsus. At that, feelings of relief sprang up in our hearts. We knew then that since a near company of our soldiers stood just beyond the river, no attack could be afoot.

In Tarsus, I learned of the conversion of Paul to Christianity. Ignatius explained that Paul, then known as Saul, was a leading Jewish persecutor of Christians, and on the day of his conversion to Christianity had asked the high priest of his order for letters to make arrests in the synagogues in Damascus of any men and women found there belonging to the Way of Jesus. The letters would allow him to take Jesus Followers as prisoners to Jerusalem for persecution. On the journey, as Saul approached Damascus, suddenly a light from heaven flashed around him. He fell to the ground. Ignatius claimed that Paul heard a voice speak to him. "Saul! Saul!" the voice said. "Why are you opposing Me?"

"Who are You, Lord?" Saul supposedly said.

"I am Jesus," the voice replied. "I am the one you are opposing. Now, get up and go into the city. There you will be told what to do."

The men traveling with Saul, Ignatius said, stood there in fear and awe, unable to speak. They had heard the sound, but they didn't see anyone. Saul got up from the ground and opened his eyes, but he couldn't see. So his men led him by the hand to Damascus. Blind for three days, Saul neither ate nor drank anything. In Damascus, a believer named Ananias received a call from the Lord in a vision telling him to go to a certain house on a particular street and to ask for a man from Tarsus. "He is praying, and in a vision, he has seen a man named Ananias, who will place hands on him and he will be able to see again."

Ananias complained to God, Ignatius continued, that he had heard many reports on this man Saul, that he had done great harm to God's people, and that he had, under the highest Jewish authority, come to Damascus previously to arrest any he found there who worshipped Christ.

But the Lord said to Ananias, "Go! I have chosen this man to carry My name to those who are not Jews and to their kings. He will bring My name to the people of Israel. I will show him how much he must suffer for Me. Then, Ananias went to the house and entered it. He placed his hands on Saul, saying to him, "You saw the Lord Jesus. He appeared to you on the road coming here. He has sent me so that you may have your sight returned. You will be filled with the

Holy Spirit." Right away, something like scales fell from Saul's eyes, and he could see again. He got up and was baptized as a believer in Jesus Christ as Messiah. He ate and regained his strength. Then, God changed his name to Paul. After that, he went out into the synagogues, teaching that Jesus is the Son of God, to the amazement of all who heard him. And despite threats from the high priests who had licensed him to kill Way Followers, he boldly declared himself now one of them, leading legions to worship the Lord Jesus.

Ignatius said that Paul authored his favorite Scriptures, including the one he had read at his Antioch church, and that those Scriptures served as the design of his ministry.

Ignatius's passionate delivery of his story about Paul showed that he unquestionably believed it, but I did not, and as my men drifted away, none of them expressed to me that they believed him either. In fact, most of my men didn't even stay around long enough to hear it all, and it seemed to me the sentimental ramblings of an old fool desperately peddling an impossible story.

Yet as I rested alone, I found myself pondering other questions. "What does it mean to love death more than this life?" I oddly asked myself, thinking of the Communion service back in Antioch and of the Paul story. "Why not a more glorious, more heroic end for Paul than a tragic beheading in Rome?" The same end to which Ignatius would come? "Why does Ignatius say that the Lord told Paul that He would let him know how much he must suffer for the Lord? If this love of which he speaks means suffering, then why should men desire it?"

We left Tarsus without permitting Ignatius to meet with any members of his cult there, because my men continued to suspect that fanatics, inspired by Paul's memory, might create problems for our mission. I found Ignatius's stoic quietness unsettling. Still refusing to eat on a regular schedule, riding in his wagon, sleeping, and praying and telling stories of Jesus aloud—forcing us to hear, rattled and irritated me. At intervals, he would adopt a posture of stoic quietness, confounding and disturbing me as to his health. Either way, I found myself drawn to carefully study him.

Along the way to Tarsus, we discussed the path our trip should take from there, for two courses presented themselves—a path along the sea to the most populated Christian areas, the path Ignatius wanted to take, or a path that avoided these populations. We decided to bypass the potential hotbeds of the large number of Christians in Magnesia and especially in Ephesus, the latter the location of which Ignatius called the "Mother Christian Church" in Asia, the base church from which Paul spread the Gospel of Jesus in Asia over a two-year period. It raised security issues for the size and reported fervor of the Christian community there. On the other hand, the city of Laodicea, a place reported to be filled with rich, lukewarm Christians, presented a more appealing alternative. That decided, we started the long slog to Laodicea. From there we would travel north and east through Hierapolis and Sardis, and finally to Smyrna. In Smyrna, we would permit Ignatius to visit with Christian leaders and fellow members of his church in a more controlled environment.

The long shadow and influence of Paul's work on our journey's path proved inescapable. Ignatius proved a walking history lesson on the subject of Paul and Christianity. "All praises to God," he proclaimed, as he discovered that we would go through Laodicea. "Paul brought Christianity to the people of Laodicea and these nearby cities of Colossae and Hierapolis. With Epaphroditus, a Philippian, Paul founded churches and spread the knowledge of Jesus throughout that area. Paul's letter to the Colossians (residents of Colossae) praised them for their "love" of the saints, and the hope they had laid up in heaven, based on their acceptance of the truth of the gospel and its fruitfulness."

As we approached Laodicea, Ignatius asked, "To honor the spirit of Paul and his good work in the region, permit me to dismount this wagon and walk the few miles left before we would enter Laodicea."

"If you dismount this wagon, you will not be permitted to get back in it if you tire," I coldly yelled out to him. "Your choice."

He popped out of the wagon, smiling and joyous.

Hierapolis sat on a limestone hill, visible from the spot where Ignatius started his walk, looking north, across the Lycus Valley. To his southwest, we and Ignatius could also see the mound in the City of Colossae, standing seventy-five feet above that valley. Here, in this area, Christianity waged a running battle with the Greek and Roman gods; Apollo, the chief deity of Hierapolis and Colossae; and Zeus, the father of Greek gods, and his counterpart, Jupiter, in Roman religion. Temples to these gods were present throughout the area. Ignatius broke his silence, telling us that he'd also asked to walk into Laodicea in order to trample on the heads of these false gods, symbolically putting them under his Lord's feet as he trod, replacing idol worship with the love for Jesus Christ. Ignatius did not mention that he figuratively trampled on the deity called Trajan as well.

"Throw the old troll back in the wagon," Publius screamed angrily. "Is there no end to his blasphemy?" My other men shouted him down as well, railing against his obstinate denigration of our gods—Juno, Jupiter, and Apollo. I felt certain it would have been difficult for me to restrain them from doing physical harm to him, should he have questioned the deity of Emperor Trajan in his tirade. Yet shout and debase him as we might, Ignatius persisted in praising his God, his Jesus. Finally, reaching the city's boundaries, he tired and asked to ride in his wagon.

"Request denied," I happily shouted out, to the delight of my men, who vociferously cheered me on. We taunted him through the city limits, and decided to add the further indignity of having him hobble all the way to our night's lodging place. I only regretted that night had fallen and our display of deserved cruelty to Ignatius could not be more openly witnessed by more people.

But we shouted his name and circumstances out to all who would listen, taking terms announcing: "He who is in chains is the fabled Ignatius, Bishop of the Christian church of Antioch. Remember Antioch! It was the place where we first gave this cult of Jesus followers the derisive name "Christians!" Unlawful Christians. Atheist Christians. We created that name. Sadly, they appropriated it; and now we will destroy it. Remember Antioch! Ignatius, head of the Christian Club, is doomed to die in Rome. All hail Emperor Trajan, God of Rome!

We stayed in Laodicea for another week, making the final decision there to permit all the meetings with church leaders in Smyrna. Our stay was quiet, with the men getting the opportunity to rest. However, for Ignatius it was pure torment, as my men went before him continually raising praises to the Greek and Roman gods and our Emperor and denouncing Jesus as a fraud and Ignatius with Him. Ignatius was happy to move on toward Smyrna, but we determined to cause him to suffer more of the same there.

Smyrna's impressive outline struck us as we approached it. Situated on the slopes of Mount Pagos, Smyrna overlooked the Gulf of Izmir. Built on flat land around the harbor on the road between Ephesus and Pergamum, it was only around thirty-five miles from Ephesus—making for an easy journey for the church leaders from there and the cities in proximity to it. Its population of around two hundred thousand people rivaled that of Ephesus, but compared to Ephesus, it was far more steeped in pagan and secular traditions. Homer, the great Greek poet, was born there, and shrines in his honor greeted guests to the wonderful libraries in the city. The temple of the Mother Goddess stood near the harbor. Particularly obnoxious to Ignatius, this temple housed numerous other temples of the imperial cults, or the cults of emperor worship. This reason also justified our choosing Smyrna as the place to take a respite from our taxing journey before continuing to our final destination—to linger in a place whose temples and shrines would again daily vex Ignatius.

A few days after arriving in Smyrna, I permitted Ignatius to send messengers to the churches at Ephesus, Magnesia, and Tralles. Officials from these churches started arriving shortly thereafter. Under Emperor Trajan's enlightened policy, Christians didn't have to hide their identity or face persecution, they simply had not to act seditiously or suspiciously, and certainly had to avoid openly insulting the gods of Rome. That had been Ignatius's failing, in principal part, the other being his apparent arrogance, insulting Trajan. Were that not the case, then these leaders of the Christian Church could not have visited openly with Ignatius. But after observing their enthusiastic embrace of Ignatius, so powerful were these scenes that I started to believe they would have braved the threat of arrest and torture to sit with him. We turned away many desiring to visit with him. However, the Ephesus delegation, headed by their bishop, Onesimus, I felt compelled to have visit Ignatius first, both because it was the largest church that made request and because it seemed the ripest for our information-gathering aims about the work and habits of these so-called Christians.

Bishop Onesimus of the Ephesus church had in his company his deacons Burrhus, Crocus, and Euplius, and a layman, Fronto. None dressed ostentatiously, but arrived in fine attire and spoke and acted as men of authority and of some training. Ignatius and these men greeted each other with kisses and tears.

"The sight of you in chains, Ignatius, oh, grand priest of God, sinks my heart to utter despair. I suffered the chains of slavery in my youth, a slavery from which I physically escaped, and the service of which I hated. My running from that slavery led me to encounter Paul in my travels, and he introduced me to the liberating influence of Jesus Christ, which has led to both my physical and my spiritual freedom to this day. But even in my darkest days of bondage as a slave, I did not feel the pain and sorrow for myself that I now feel for you—seeing you in these unnecessary and disgusting chains. You're an old man. How far and how fast could you run? Do these men know nothing of your godly royalty? Your honesty? That you would not commit a crime or run away if they unloosed you? Oh, Ignatius, I am so sorry. And your garments? Must they shame you in dress as well?" Onesimus cried, tears streaming uncontrollably.

"Now, now, my dear brother bishop. I know that you are sincerely hurting for me, and I truly thank you for your love—a love that runs mutually between us. But these chains make me not a slave, not a criminal, and these clothes, not a peasant and not a prisoner. The Lord Jesus Christ executes justice for the oppressed, offers food and raiment for the peasant, and gives freedom to those the state would deem prisoners. If a prisoner, then I am His, nonetheless. So cry not for me but for those who know not the Lord, perhaps for these my captors and tormentors. They are truly prisoners in every sense."

"Me, a prisoner. I am a free soldier of Rome. We will see which of us dies in Rome—at the teeth of Trajan's Lions," Publius bellowed.

"Not just you, young soldier. But any man everywhere, from the highest to the lowest, is a prisoner to sin and the devil. I pray you will come to know Jesus and find freedom."

Publius fumed, as I and the others of my men sneered in laughter.

Onesimus cleared his throat, and our attention returned to his meeting. Drying his eyes, he pleaded, "Forgive me for causing this distraction, Bishop. It is just that you did not appear as I expected, as I have ever seen you. And may God forgive me as well for my outburst. I have also been impolite in not introducing these who are with me. They are strong in the faith and are honored to meet you... to be received by you."

Onesimus described the work of each man to Ignatius, and each was warmly embraced by him.

"I know that my departure from this world is untimely in the eyes of men, even, I must admit, in my eyes to some extent, because I am at work at overcoming the many challenges that our church at Antioch faces and have been completely dedicated to dealing with them. The Antioch church is under attack from within and without, and I had felt myself a necessary person to deal with it, to rescue it and set it on a forward course—to unify and to stabilize it, as well as many other churches. But, in the end, Christ is the bishop of all of our churches, and He will work His will through us or another whom He will anoint for His kingdom's glory. He has now called me to a greater work, that I am now satisfied to perform."

"Bishop, there are some in our church at Ephesus who are rising up against Bishop Onesimus, challenging him on church doctrine, questioning whether it is even required that they follow his leadership or that of any other bishop or church leader, asking whether each may find his own way to follow after Christ...whether, in other words, the bishop is truly appointed by Christ for the proper ordering of the church. You are wise in years and experience; tell us how to best instruct them in these matters," Deacon Burrhus said.

Ignatius thought for a moment, pleased with the question and the sincerity of the deacon.

"There must be harmony between the leadership of the bishop and the followers of Jesus, for the bishops are shepherds of Christ's sheep, having been appointed according to the will of Christ for ordained leadership and divine order in His church. There must be unity, in love, and there is a godly reward in honoring the man God has placed over them. Let them know that, and that I have arrived at this position through meditation on the Scriptures, prayer, and fasting, and not only me but many other leaders of the Antioch church, beginning with St. Peter, and then St. John, who instructed me in these matters."

"You have spoken well, Ignatius. Let us pray for each other. May God strengthen you to complete this journey which I am now fully convinced He has assigned to your hands. May we be inspired by your testimony through this work to the glory of Jesus Christ for so long as He wills to keep you in this life and to be seen of men," Onesimus said humbly.

"God has well-chosen you for Ephesus, as I never doubted that He had, and that is further reason why I can leave my labors here with songs of triumph in my heart," Ignatius said.

"Please tell your church that it was my desire to visit them personally, but I was not permitted to do so by these heartless leopards. Tell them of my love and that I will write to them shortly. May God go with you."

As Bishop Onesimus and his delegation left, there were kisses again and more warm embraces. However, this time, there were no tears of sorrow or sadness for Ignatius.

The Magnesians, led by Bishop Damas and his elders and deacons, pressed their way to confer with Ignatius a few days later. Having been apprised of Ignatius's rather forsaken appearance, they took pains not to register shock on their faces in seeing him, but simply greeted him in love and thanksgiving.

"Welcome," Ignatius spouted, genuinely happy to see them, "my dear brothers in Christ. You honor me by your presence and your travel to see this wretch. Bishop Damas, I have heard of you.

That you are so young, yet so learned in Scripture and so humble in leadership is well known, and received by all of us who, well, one might say, have more than a sprinkle of gray."

They then laughed in good spirits with him, assembling around his knees, and falling into conversation with him as children before a revered and wise grandfather.

Finally, Bishop Damas waxed serious about the business at hand.

"I deserve no praise, certainly not that which you so generously gave me starting out here. I am nothing, before both God and you. I envy that God has called you to give your life for His cause, rather than me, for I would gladly take your place. Though I am young and have the prospect of years to serve God's purposes here on Earth, and may grow in stature over time, at present, you are twenty-fold abler than am I to contribute to the building up of God's church. God knows best, but through my dim eyes, the growth of His now fragile church is far better served by my death than by yours," Damas said quietly.

"Your words prove why you are so beloved, Damas. But may I take the license accorded to an old man to tell you bluntly that you are wrong? For Scripture says, if we live, we live to the Lord. If we die, we die to the Lord. Therefore, whether we live or die, as believers, we are in the Lord—none greater than another. He gives His people the leaders they need for a season, and He knows the right season for each of them...each of us. His will is right."

"Your words take my breath away, Bishop Ignatius. I have a wife and a young child. She worried that I should come and meet here in Smyrna, fearing that it was perhaps a trap by the Romans to gather all of the church leadership in our region together and to forcibly take us all to Rome for some sort of mass execution. I told her that you would not agree to receive us in that case and that we had to trust God. I was not worried for myself but for her. Had I not come, I would have forsaken an audience with Jesus, for surely, through you, He is in our midst today. I will tell her and I will tell all the others how we all must be bolder for Christ. You are much more than a wise and venerable sage of Jesus. Christ is in you, magnified more than in any man I have ever met, and His light shines around you. God reveals this to me through His Spirit."

"As He does yours to me. How goes your church, really? What are you wrestling with, other than the freshness of your face?"

"You embarrass me, sir. I am afraid I cannot get any beard to grow as fast or as full as I would like. But that challenge aside, false doctrines are rife among our people and we are kept busy batting them down. Many who have joined with us are attempting to walk in the old ways of Judaism and the new ways of Christianity at the same time. Faith through grace saves, as Christ has declared, but some still teach and some still hold to the view that the law yet is the measuring stick toward salvation—even those who manifest a sincere belief in Jesus Christ."

"Christ is the only Teacher," Ignatius said. "It is not grace and the law by which we live in Christ, for His grace is sufficient. Our righteousness is of Him, and depends on Him alone. Tell them, thus says an old priest of greater than eighty years who will soon meet the Lord. Tell them, thus said the Lord."

"Through His death—which a few still deny and cause confusion regarding—was it done as you have said. But what of those who say that He did not truly die but went home to the Father before He was crucified, and further, that He did not, could not, live as a man, for, as God, He was too Holy to do or be such a thing?" his deacon plaintively inquired.

"That is the essential mystery of our faith…that He lived among us, as a man, that He suffered and died as a man, and that He was raised from the dead through the might of the Holy Spirit. To deny that is to miss the message of Christ and to make vain the Church. Not only that, but that the same power that raised Him raised those from the dead who slept in the faith of God at the moment of His resurrection is the same promise that He makes to all of us now who believe in Him. There is no other way. There is only this one way. There is no binary path. I will send a letter to your church to instruct them further."

They went away with singing and shedding tears of joy and thanksgiving.

Bishop Polybius, Deacon Cilicia and a fellow Christian, Agathopus, from Tralles also met with Ignatius at Smyrna. Agathopus decided to stay and travel with Ignatius to Rome, to continue soaking in his wisdom and life lessons.

The Trallians sent a question to be put to Ignatius, different from those yet raised by the others: "Why would God let a man of God like you die in the terrible way that lies before you?" This question dismayed Ignatius, and he began to weep. I wondered why, and then, Ignatius spoke. "Your question completely loses focus on the things of Christ. I had rather thought you more mature in your Christian walk. I had thought you were far beyond this sort of question. You sound like despairing men who do not know Christ.

Now, Ignatius wept more. *How strange*, I thought. Ignatius reactions made me listen more closely. Gathering himself and, perhaps, his thoughts, he offered a hoarse sounding response.

"Please, please, listen. Christ died for us, that we might, through faith in Him, escape the finality of death in the natural, not that we might avoid a natural death altogether. Yet the reward is in dying for His sake. To believe otherwise is to believe false doctrine, as false as the belief in Judaism as a constant with Christianity. In Christ there is no death, only life."

"You have always taught us well in word. Now, you majestically show us, by example, that the essence of love is self-sacrifice," Polybius confessed.

"I now understand that to suffer like Christ is to be like Him."

"Jesus said that the world would know His disciples, not because of their gifts or even their miracles but by their love, one to the other. That is my ultimate message to your church: love each other as Christ has loved you, and Christ will be in your hearts and His Holy Spirit will guide you," Ignatius said. "Sacrificial suffering is born of love. For men, the ultimate sacrifice is to surrender their lives to Him. Not only unto death, as I am now called to do, but in the small, everyday deeds of their lives."

"Tell them to listen for the voice of the Holy Spirit and their ears will hear Him saying, 'This is the way, walk in it, whenever you turn to the right or the left.'"

And then they prayed together and sang hymns so sincerely that all who heard seemed touched. Indeed, I felt moved, enticed by this mystery, wanting to understand it, to know more about it. Looking around, I seemed to sense that even the most hardhearted among my men were listening, questioning what they were hearing, all of us caught up in wonderment. None of us had ever seen or heard anything like what we witnessed in these meetings, and especially this latter one.

As delegations came and went, word reached Ignatius that some Christian leaders in Rome were bargaining with the emperor to grant him a reprieve from his death sentence. Instead of being cheered by this, he became sorely agitated, and hurried to dissuade them. He urged me to have a letter delivered to the Christians in Rome as soon as possible. I read it and made notes for Crassus. It said:

> Ignatius, also known as Theophorous, to the church that has found mercy in the greatness of the Most High Father and in Jesus Christ, His only Son; to the church beloved and enlightened after the love of Jesus Christ, our God, by the will of Him who willed everything which is, I salute in the name of Jesus Christ, the Son of the Father. To those who are united in flesh and spirit and who are filtered clear of every foreign stain, I wish unalloyed joy in Jesus Christ.
>
> I desire only that I may not merely speak but also have the will, that I may be called a Christian but may also be found to be one.
>
> I go to Rome to die in the cause of Christ. I am chained to ten leopards, that is to a detachment of soldiers, who only grow worse in the face of kindness. I am writing to all the churches, and I enjoin them all that I am dying willingly for God's sake, if only you do not prevent it. I beg of you, do not do me an untimely kindness. Allow me to be eaten by the beasts, which are my way

of reaching God. I am God's wheat and I am to be ground by the teeth of the wild beasts so that I will become the pure bread of Christ. Not as Peter and Paul do I commend you. They were apostles, and I am a convict. They were free, and I even to the present time am a slave. Yet, if I suffer, I shall be the freedman of Jesus Christ, and in Him I shall rise up free. Now in chains, I am learning to have no desires of my own.

I have no taste for corruptible food nor for the pleasures of life. I desire the bread of God, which is the flesh of Jesus Christ, who was the seed of David, and for drink His blood, which is love incorruptible.

By this short letter, I beg you to believe me. Jesus Christ will make it clear to you that I am speaking the truth. He is the mouth that cannot lie, by which the Father has spoken truly.

I shared Ignatius's letter with some of my men. I tried to read their reactions to it. I was struggling with my own. I tried not to reveal this to them outright, but they were sensing something affecting me.

"You can't be beginning to take this duped man seriously, now, can you, Aurelius?" Marius, my best friend among them, asked, with a worried look on his face.

I paused before answering him, searching his face and those of the others. Everything in Ignatius's letter was about goodness and love, about exhorting his followers to steadfastness and unity in the pursuit of their cause. Some of it, frankly, struck me as uplifting. Unsure of how a comment along those lines would be received, I avoided answering Marius directly, focusing his, if not their, attention away from things aroused in my heart.

"Whatever do you think he meant, calling us leopards in his letter? I'm sure he did not mean to flatter us by the use of that term," I said.

"It should come to you as no surprise that our prisoner would call us names. After all, we are not taking him for a walk in the city square; rather, we are walking him to his death, and a very horrible death besides," Marius offered.

"Yes," I responded to Marius, "but he continues to speak of forgiveness for us, calling on his God to forgive us and even the emperor. That, you must admit, is surprising. That would not be my reaction. It's not natural."

"I know a little about leopards," Publius, adding his two quadrans to the mix, interjected. "They are fierce, solitary hunters. Once they taste a man's blood, they become hunters of men, more dangerous than a lion in that respect. When their jaws seize prey, nothing can loosen them, neither lance nor gladius. I encountered them in many of my campaigns in Lebanon and in Africa. Another thing I should say, though, that may give clearer meaning to Ignatius's reference to us as leopards, is that African witch doctors crave their spotted coats. They claim their spots are immutable, one of the few things in the world that can be depended on to never change—like immortals of another world. The witch doctors cover their backs with leopard hides, believing in the leopard's power to protect them and to make their medicines powerful and consistently trustworthy."

"Nonsense. Pure nonsense!" I answered. "Truly he does not think us immortals. Insisting upon the existence of only one immortal God and one Son of God, Jesus, is what is costing him his life and costing us an unwelcomed trip to Rome. It must be the latter reason. He thinks we are too evil to change, so evil we will not return kindnesses. So evil that, like the leopard, we cannot change our ways—our spots. Perhaps, that is what he means," I reasoned.

"Well, Aurelius," Marius said, laughing, "then Ignatius should call himself a leopard, too. He's an obstinate ass."

"Perhaps," I responded, smiling with him, though I wasn't convinced. Marius's description of Ignatius did not quite seem to fit him. Sure of his God, unflinching in his faith, yes. Yet I did not see evil in him. It took both of these qualities to make a leopard. More likely Ignatius saw both in us.

"I found it peculiar that he should express a zeal to be thrown to the beasts. Not a lack of fear only but a zeal—for a grotesque death. Did you?" Marius asked, shaking his head.

"Madness! Plain madness!" Antonius chimed in. "That is what is unnatural. By our very nature, men desire to live, to fight to live. We will to survive. Anything else is lunacy, and Ignatius, a lunatic! We make ourselves the same by trying to make sense out of what is nonsensical." Then he stood up.

"Good night, my friends. Let's douse the lanterns and get some rest. Who knows what challenges we may face tomorrow? We must be sure not to let our guard down by studying our prisoner with sympathy."

Standing up to leave our meeting, I agreed.

"Good night, all," I called out. "Tomorrow!"

I noticed Marius observing me, as if he wanted to continue searching my mind on the subject he'd raised. With my joining with Antonius, though, all headed to their sleeping quarters.

I walked to the front doors of the barracks to make sure our sentries remained posted as assigned, and found them in place. I went to my bed. As head of our troop, I enjoyed the privilege of sleeping in a private room. I did not sleep well. Too many questions spun in my head. I arose and walked over to Ignatius's cell. Kneeling and praying over the two of my men who slept, still chained to him, in his cell, his face seemed aglow in the moonlight and tracked with tears. Was he praying for them?

CHAPTER 4
A LONGING

*"For he satisfieth the longing soul, and filleth the
hungry soul with goodness."*
—*Psalm 107:9 (KJV)*

Ignatius's letters and the events in the cell that I had witnessed two nights before left me more than intrigued. My curiosity about Ignatius and his Jesus Followers grew daily. It filled me with questions and consumed me in dreams and wonderings. I could not explain the source of these odd ruminations.

"Who is this strange figure of a man calling himself Bishop Ignatius?" I asked myself. "Bishop Ignatius of the church of the one and only true God, no less? A follower, no, a leader, of the Followers of Jesus, the Son of God, the Way, the Messiah? How frail is this pitiable personage standing against the power of the Roman Empire, indeed having done so in the presence of Emperor Trajan, making audacious claims of the imminence of his God to the most powerful man on Earth? Did he not know that Emperor Trajan would snatch the life out of him as quickly as a frog flashes out his tongue to catch a fly, an act for which Trajan, as a god, answers to no one? Who can save this pathetic priest? For his blatant obstinacy, who should even try to save him? And, by Hercules, why is he not calling on the God of his strength to come forth and deliver him? The Jews, from whence his cult springs, make sacrifices to Emperor Trajan and to the Empire for their success and sustenance. Why, then, the perversity of these Christians, of this Ignatius, in not rendering libations to Trajan?"

So I said to myself, "Enough!" But after promising in the previous night's sleeplessness that I would not be vexed by Ignatius's predicament, I was, nevertheless, still troubled the next day. Try as I might to sincerely perish my thoughts of him, some unexplainable force drew them toward him, rendering me unable to avert my eyes and mind from him.

"By Jupiter," I protested over and over in my solitude, "this Jesus is just a fomenter of a superstition. Look at the miserable band of riffraff following closely onto Ignatius, caught up in this Jesus contagion, this insanity. This talk of Jesus, a resurrected Messiah, is the drivel of fools!"

Would that I could have cast Ignatius out of my presence, my mind, my sight! But I could not, for, under orders of Emperor Trajan, my men were literally chained to him, as I was figuratively, by chains of iron, until we had fed him to the lions in the Roman Coliseum.

"I will resist Ignatius's magic! I will not be hypnotized by him," I shouted deep inside. "I will forbid him to speak to me and my men about his god. Let him be alone with his miserable god!"

In a few days, new intrusions invaded my thoughts. For two nights, I dreamed a frightening and unsettling dream. In it, I became a follower of Ignatius's god. I pledged my belief in Jesus. How absurd! "I don't believe in Jesus!" I declared. Perhaps, my dreams are betraying me because, as a soldier, always depending on courage, I was just drawn to search for the source of Ignatius's courage. Thus, the following morning I made an unspoken declaration: "I desire that the God of Ignatius show me a sign that He is as Ignatius claims. I...I demand a sign!"

But what would I do if one appeared? I was perplexed to the point of fearing for the soundness of my mind! In my brief dream, I became one of them, one of a multitude of them. Emperor Trajan directed me to curse Jesus and renounce Him and I would not! I could not. How could that ever be?

Trying to bring myself under control, I mused that, perhaps, my dreams and thoughts were sympathetic feelings for a foolish old man, needlessly throwing away his life. Or maybe it was a sorcerer's power that Ignatius possessed that enthralled me. But I was, in any case, consumed with expectation, even perhaps the hope, of a sign—outward, tangible evidence that might vindicate Ignatius on the one hand and that would prove that my dream was not sophistry on the other. A sign like the one Ignatius explained that Paul received on his way to persecute Christians—a sign that caused his conversion. Yet I deny to the gods that I sought a conversion! I found myself sitting up in my bed screaming out to an empty room, "I do not seek a conversion!"

"I am seeking only evidence confirming the truth, or not, of Jesus," I said, calming down. "It's just my native curiosity."

That was all that I allowed myself to think. For if indeed, a light shone around Paul, and Jesus called him into His following, then why not some sign for me? I needed a sign, not an aborted, sketchy dream to figure this thing out!

I had to remind myself that I was Aurelius Maximus, a soldier of the Roman Empire, and at present commanding officer of the emperor's special troop to deliver Ignatius to meet his death sentence in Rome. I had witnessed the reverence and emotions he generated among the leaders and followers of his cult. However, I had been trained to always carry myself with discipline and correctness. I was obligated by religious tradition to uphold the beliefs I had been taught about the immortal gods that had come down to me from my state and my ancestors. I was sworn never to permit any eloquence, pity, sympathy, or other emotion or concern to dislodge me from the tenets of my inherited religion and the obligations of my sworn duty.

I held the conviction that Romulus, by his auspices, and Numa, by his establishment of sacred rituals, laid the foundations of our state, and that our state was great because of the divine favor of our gods. We believed in numerous gods: Jupiter (father of gods), Juno (His wife and guardian of marriage), Mars (god of war), Venus (goddess of love and beauty), Mercury (messenger of the gods), Neptune (god of water, sea, and earthquakes), and other lesser gods, who involved themselves in our affairs and protected us, not as individuals but as families and as a state. Other, separate gods we added to meet peculiar or particular needs as they arose throughout life. We even adopted the gods of people we conquered, when we thought they might be helpful. Perhaps this Jesus might be a special god to me, separate from the others, for me, maybe a new god of courage. This might explain my current burning desire to search for Him—not to replace the god of my fathers but to fill a new need. In this way, I might stand in two worlds, that of my present gods and that of the god of Ignatius, should I see the need to choose Him. I doubted that I might ever be ready to abandon my obligations to the gods of my ancestors. How could one god be more idyllic for any man than can many gods, anyway? How could a dead carpenter, a crucified carpenter, be more than, at best, a dead prophet? Not a resurrected savior of the souls of men!

Though these thoughts competed, I found myself still dwelling on a hope for a miraculous sign of some sort from Ignatius's god. After all, who was Paul compared to me? My musings for a sign were justified, as I counted the magnitude of my crimes (if one could rightly call what I had done in the name of the emperor and the Empire crimes) in rooting out what I and the state believed were acts of sedition by Christians. By my proofs, I had been more zealous in this regard than was Paul. I held a position of authority that made it so. I enthusiastically raided the houses and assemblies of Christians, with the authority not to bring an offending one to a Jewish High Priest, which was the limit of Paul's authority, but to plunge a spear or dagger into the heart of any resister or fanatic. I had done that many times. Paul acted as a mere go-between. Having eclipsed Paul in the number and severity of my incursions upon and assaults against Christians, was it unreasonable for me to expect my own supernatural substantiation?

If not a miracle of Jesus awesomely appearing accompanied by lights and angels, as for Paul, then surely Jesus would manifest Himself as Messiah through a particular feeling that would come upon me—a sensation that would overwhelm me. Should I not lose control of my senses and speech or be swept away in a flood of tears of joy and gratitude? Or should I not tremble, faint away, or, bent at the waist, wail, stricken in a swoon or reduced to a state of apparent drunkenness, like I had witnessed countless simple so-called Christians do?

Important to me was the need for certainty in this matter, for I had a lot to lose—a soldier's career, an enviable one, indeed, to lose. Though I could have started higher, I began as a common soldier, in the consulate, at the age of twenty-one. I fought bravely and aggressively with the single-minded purpose of annihilating any enemy set before me. For my courage and loyalty, I gained command of a company of spearman. Refusing to accept discharges, though sustaining serious wounds in battle, I volunteered repeatedly for additional service. Emperor Trajan, on the recommendation of my commanders and the history of my valor in the Dacian and Parthian wars, gave me charge of securing him in the region of Central Asia Minor, and also of the forts of that region, protecting the major cities of Iconium, Lystra, Perga, and Antioch of Syria. Now having completed twenty years of valiant and unblemished service, I had earned the respect of my superiors, my colleagues, and Emperor Trajan himself. Perhaps most importantly, I had the respect of my father, who was himself a centurion, head of a Roman legion, serving under Emperor Trajan as a military leader before he became emperor. Though in some ways my military achievements had surpassed my father's, I still humbly submitted to his tutelage and craved his acceptance and approval. Could I risk abandoning everything I had sacrificed to earn as a soldier of the Empire to follow this New Way? Should I risk falling from the ranks of the persecutors to the persecuted to follow the Way without an unmistakable mystical sign? Could I possibly risk ruining the favor I enjoyed with my father? Could I abandon the gods who had favored me?

That these questions cluttered my mind deeply surprised me. Why was I so hopelessly troubled? By Jupiter or by Jesus, I needed a sign!

We remained in Smyrna for more than a week with Ignatius. Church leaders and Jesus followers continuously clamored to visit him and bask in his presence. Observing their passionate behavior toward him, made me wonder more about this strange tugging at my heart to know what caused this outpouring of love and respect. Curiously, I began to feel something almost akin to jealousy toward my men who were chained to Ignatius. I usually stood a distance from him, riding in my chariot during the days when we traveled or in my office on the days we were in barracks, and sleeping apart from him and my men at night. While I was near him when he met with the leaders from Ephesus and Tralleaus, my men were constantly in close proximity to him and could speak with him and listen to his talks with others daily, hourly. Desiring to spend some time with him, perhaps to search out my dreams, I determined to seek a justification to have him chained to me, if only for one night. I mulled the thought that perhaps I could disguise my motives by telling the men that they were having all the fun with him and that I wished to intimidate him and make him miserable by requiring that he be brought into my presence. Perhaps, I thought, I could say that joining him to me in chains would afford the opportunity for me to study him up close and firsthand, to investigate him and his motives, as it were—maybe to win his trust and delve into the secrets of his Jesus cult. Perhaps I could say to my men that chaining myself to him would be my effort to lead by example, doing this distasteful thing myself that was now only theirs to do, to walk in their shoes. Then I came to my senses. As the commander of this troop of ten, I owed them no excuse or explanation. They would have their questions, but why should that matter? I would take the measures that appeared necessary to me to shake the feeling, the near hunger, to hear from him, to experience him. I would assert my prerogative as commander confidently, explaining nothing to my men.

"Antonius, Minucius, you will be relieved of your obligation to sleep chained to Ignatius tonight. I will take that responsibility and personally guard him through the night."

"But, sir," Antonius began protesting. Holding up my hand, I thwarted it.

"I insist. I insist and that is the end of it."

Nearing bedtime, I stripped myself of my uniform and donned a tunic and a nightcap for sleeping. When I arrived at the enclosure where Ignatius was locked away for the night, with Antonius and Minucius chained to him, each stood to salute me. This destroyed any slight chance that existed that Ignatius would not recognize me as captain of the command. I do not know why that foolish hope entered my head. Perhaps, I dared not admit, I felt a certain conscious awe of him and the need to hide my true self from him.

"I'll take it from here, men. Good night. Rouse me at the usual time," I commanded. "Leave these keys with me. I will fasten this to my wrist."

"Are you certain, sir—certain that at least one of us should not remain with you?"

"Nonsense! He's but a weak old man, over eighty years old, with only his fists and his feet to attack me. I should be laughed out of the emperor's army, let alone this command, were I not able to repel him. Do either of you doubt me in that?" I laughed. Laughing along with me, my men made their way to their sleeping quarters. What they truly thought of my behavior that night, I knew not and cared not.

Holding the chains Ignatius wore while sleeping, I realized their heaviness, for they were made of thick iron. They were affixed to both Ignatius's wrists and ankles with wrist and ankle bracelets. These were not the chains he wore during daylight hours. Their weight surprised me.

Quite a burden they must be to this old man, I thought to myself, as I dragged the chains across the floor to a mat near Ignatius that would be his bed for the night.

"Would you like me to loosen your leg chains, Ignatius?"

"No, Captain. But thank you. Though I am an old man, I am stronger than you think. I'm past worrying about these chains. I am, in fact, happy to carry these small burdens for my Lord." He turned away, saying nothing more.

I felt chastened.

"Have you enough food and water on this journey?"

"Quite enough," he said, sitting up straight, as if bothered by my question. "Were the quality of the food and drink matched by the character of your men, I would be quite satisfied. As you have seen, I have been subjected to the foulest treatment by nearly all of them. They have recently stopped jerking my chains to induce me to awkward missteps or falls, accompanied by their roaring laughter. Maybe that ceased to amuse them—or maybe I took it without complaining and it gave them no satisfaction. They act as an adolescent mob, ferocious in looks, coarse in language, but altogether unpersuasive as mature men. Soldiers of Rome? The finest? But why tell you of these things? You have seen and tolerated them. Indeed, you have been party to some of these bad actions against me. Forgive me for wasting your time." And, with that, he reclined back onto the floor of his cell.

In my heart, I was forced to admit that he was right.

A few minutes passed. Then, I asked, "Would you like my mat to rest upon tonight? I will sleep on the floor."

Looking stunned, Ignatius answered, "If you would please it so. Yes."

"Then, here, take it."

"You may want to think twice about this noble act, Captain. I've become used to sleeping without creature comforts. But what will your men think of you giving yours to me, you a Roman soldier, sharing with me?"

"They answer to me. Here, take the mat," I said, pushing it roughly over near Ignatius and directing him to lie on it. "And I will loosen your leg chains."

Ignatius pulled the mat closer and rolled onto it. I unlocked his leg chains, and Ignatius sighed deeply, feeling the softness of the mat and the comfort of the freedom of his legs. He lay there, praying openly for a moment, thanking God for touching my heart to render him these small kindnesses. Then, he asked me a question.

"To whom do you pray, Captain?"

Taken aback, I sputtered, "Are you trying to offend me after my show of kindness?"

"Why do you ask?"

Not allowing him time to answer, I shot back my own insulting question.

"Do you seek to pray to my gods before resting?" I mocked him. "Is that why you ask, Ignatius?"

Ignatius laughed.

"No. You should know better by now. I take that as a jest," he said. "But the question I asked you just occurred to me, for I do not know what or in whom you believe. I meant no harm by it. It need not be answered. There is only one true and living God, and His Son is Jesus Christ, my Redeemer. If you do not pray to Him, then you pray in vain."

This appeared a challenge to me. Never one to back down from a challenge, I engaged him.

"I have fought many battles for the Roman Empire. I have come through terrible battles and come out largely unscathed. For that, and for my power and victory in battle, I owe the god Mars. I honor him with sacrifices before battle and share with him the spoils of triumph. I also honor the military standards bearing the image of my Divine Emperor, Trajan. I swear by the standards and place my trust in them, my emperor, and the State of Rome. These are my traditions and those of my fathers."

Ignatius closed his eyes and prayed. Shocked by his lack of response, I grew anxious in the silence and started up again.

"Minerva. There is also Minerva whom I worship, the goddess of the intellectual aspect of war. The war plans for which I enjoy some fame she has provided me wisdom to make. Minerva is the daughter of Jupiter, the king of the gods, the Best and the Greatest. I pray to her as well," I found himself muttering, almost defensively.

"So many gods," Ignatius finally sighed. "Tell me, do any of them remove your fear of death?"

I struggled to comprehend the question.

"I am a soldier of Rome. I do not fear death. I engage in battle willingly, aggressively, leading in battle, exposing my ribs to swords, lances, and arrows that could mean death. No. I am not afraid to die." Then, I said more loudly, "I am not afraid to die for Rome," wondering at the same time why I even answered that question.

"With respect," Ignatius responded, "that was not my question. Permit me to try again. "Do you expect to live after your earthly death? For if you do not, then I submit that despite your bravery, you fear the unknown on the other side of death."

"What is this riddle?" I asked. "After death, according to my beliefs, I will become a shadow, walking unseen among men, helping my descendants where I might. That is my belief." That was the way it was, I thought to myself. "That is…"

"Do your gods love you?" Ignatius asked, before I could finish my thoughts on his latest question.

"They reward me. They protect me. They..."

"But, Captain, do they love you?"

"That concept is not a part of my relationship with the gods of my tradition. That question makes no sense!" I answered sharply.

"A god who loves you, loves you unconditionally, would provide life, indeed a better life, in the one that follows. He would not leave you to walk around in darkness throughout eternity. He would not let you perish for all existence after a brief stint on this earth. My God loves me so much that He sent His Son to die for me, for my sins, as the perfect sacrifice, so that through Him, I could become righteous and spotless like Him, so that I would be fit to have a glorious life with Him in a perfect place forever, when this life is over. That is the connection between God's love for me and my lack of fear of death. That is why I have asked these two questions of you in succession."

I looked upon Ignatius's face, which exuded confidence and peace, and that sight and Ignatius's words began to shake the firmness of the foundations of my beliefs and the desires of my life.

"There is no fear in love, Captain. Perfect love, as is the love of my God, casts out fear. Invite Him to let His love into your heart, and He will. Even for you and your men. Good night, Captain."

Then, Ignatius curled up on his mat and slept. But I could not.

I unloosed myself from Ignatius's chains and went to my quarters to retrieve my papyrus, upon which to write. Then, I put it down. But, the next evening, I took it up again, this time finishing it. My letter read:

> Dear Father,
>   I am anxious about things regarding which I need your guidance. These matters are not about the things of war. I have lived frugally, scrupulously, and piously. My earliest recollections are of you sacrificing to the gods in our household as we assembled for meals, births, marriages, even puberty cele-

brations. I have placated the gods as you taught me. Near the entrance of my home, at the lararium that you built there for me, I have made supplication to the gods to watch over and protect my home and my goings and comings. I have recognized these rituals as not only coming from you but passed down from our fathers and from the Divine Emperor, Augustus, himself. I have rendered abundant gifts to the gods from the spoils of battle, believing, as you taught, that the more abundant the gift to the gods, the more acceptable it would be to them. I had not considered the thought, until now, that it may not be the quantity of the gift to the gods but the quality of the heart of the one offering the gift that counts most.

I do not want to dishonor you by even the thought of departing from the principle that you have so deeply engrained in me and by which all Romans live, embodied in the expression, "It is not done in Rome." But, dear Father, I have questions tonight that this tenet does not truly answer or even address. Can it be that there is one God whose presence is not symbolized by statues and temples built with public funds and in rituals and ceremonies sponsored or designed by emperors? Is this thought that I ponder blasphemy or disloyalty to the state or a pricking of my conscience toward the truth? Suppose this God can bring greater favor to Rome? Could I still be considered disloyal if that is my motive in searching Him out? Forgive me for these questions. I could not sleep without telling you of my yearning deep inside to know more about the God, the Jesus, of this Bishop Ignatius, whom I am duty-bound to deliver to meet his death in the Coliseum in Rome for his insolence to Emperor Trajan. Before now, I have thought Ignatius a mad man to speak of his death in Rome as gain, as entry into everlasting life with a resurrected Jesus Christ. The greater mystery of this man is that he is not brave in the sense that you and I are in facing or defying death for our state. Rather, he believes that death is nothing. And not only him but many other men, appearing as sane as are we, believe the same. Can we, either of us, say that we would not prefer our lives in this world as soldiers of Rome to those as shadows in the next? But they prefer death, rather than life here with family and friends, if their death is for the sake of Jesus Christ. So, I can no longer say with absolute certainty that the belief in one all-powerful, loving, invisible God is a fool's fantasy. Above all, I am not certain that that belief is a scandal or a threat to Rome.

I beg your patience. I am your son and I thought you should know what is on my heart that is causing me such angst. Please, I need your careful advice, as always.

With respect, your son,
Aurelius, Captain of the
Emperor's Guard in Syria

The conviction to write my father grew immediately from my conversation and observation of Ignatius that night that I lay chained to him. But looking back, the desire to search the things of his faith started from our beginning travels, added to from his meetings with church leaders along our travels, and from letters he subsequently wrote to these leaders that, of course, I read, including letters to the church in Rome. Here in Smyrna, when I permitted him to meet with the delegations from Ephesus, Magnesia, and Tralles, I witnessed delegations made up of elegant men. These men chose not to dress as simply as Ignatius, though not extravagantly, but more as men of station. The Ephesus delegation, headed by Bishop Onesimus, a former slave, converted through Paul's preaching and stewardship, was particularly impressive. Though Onesimus was once a slave, Ignatius received him in love, equally with the others. He sat humbly, but joyfully at Ignatius's feet, raptly receiving instructions along with his elders and deacons.

To the church in Ephesus, Ignatius wrote, in part:

> There is one physician who is both flesh and spirit, born and not born, who is God and man, true life in death, both from Mary and from God, first able to suffer and then unable to suffer, Jesus Christ Our Lord.
>
> I have learned, however, that certain persons from elsewhere who have evil doctrine have stayed with you; but you did not allow them to sow it among you, and you stopped your ears so that you would not receive what they sow. Your faith is what pulls you up, and love is the road that leads you to God...
>
> Do not err, my brethren: the corrupters of families will not inherit the Kingdom of God. And if they who do these things according to the flesh suffer death, how much more if a man corrupt by evil teaching the faith of God, for the sake of which Jesus Christ was crucified? A man who becomes so foul will depart into unquenchable fire; and so also will anyone who listens to him...

To the Magnesians, he wrote:

> Take care to do all things in harmony with God, with the bishop...entrusted with the business of Jesus Christ, who was with the Father in the beginning and is at last made manifest.

Do not be led astray by other doctrines nor by old fables which are worthless... Be convinced of the birth and of the passion of the resurrection, which took place during the time of the procuratorship of Pontius Pilate. These things were truly and certainly done by Jesus Christ, our hope, from which may none of you be turned aside.

Take care, therefore, to be confirmed in the decrees of the Lord of the Apostles, in order that in everything you do, you may prosper in body and soul, in faith and love, in Son and in Father and in Spirit...

And to the Trallians, he wrote, in part:

I have received the exemplar of your love and have it with me in the person of your bishop. His very demeanor is a great lesson, and his meekness is his strength. I believe that even the godless respect him.

He that is within the sanctuary is pure; but he that is outside the sanctuary is not pure. In other words, anyone who acts without the bishop and the presbytery and the deacons does not have a clear conscience.

Turn a deaf ear, then, when anyone speaks to you apart from Jesus Christ, who was of the family of David and of Mary, who was truly born, who ate and drank, was truly persecuted under Pontius Pilate, was truly crucified and died in the sight of those in heaven and on earth and in the underworld, who was also truly raised from the dead when His Father raised Him up. And, in the same manner, His Father will raise us up in Christ Jesus, if we believe in Him without whom we have no hope.

I shared these letters with Marius, but, not the one I'd had written to my father. I found him affected by Ignatius's letters, by Ignatius's visitors, and by Ignatius, as was I.

"He asked me to pray to His God, to Jesus Christ, to accept Him and He would accept me and give me eternal life with Him and freedom from earthly cares, even death," I told Marius.

"And, what happens then? What if you do pray to Him, if, if... we did?" Marius asked, in childlike wonderment.

I did not know how to answer him, so I embraced him and told him that I loved him.

CHAPTER 5
A FATHER'S CHOICE

*"Think not that I am come to send peace on earth:
I came not to send peace, but a sword. For I am
come to set a man at variance against his father...
He that loveth [his] father...more than me is not
worthy of me... And, he that taketh not take his
cross, and followeth after me, is not worthy of me."*
—*Matthew 10:34–35, 37, 38 (KJV)*

I fearfully awaited my father's response to my letter. I would have
rather spoken to him in person, so that I could parcel out my questions and thoughts to him and adjust my dosages of my ideas with
him based on his reactions. But he, living in the Arabian Peninsula,
to which he retired, left us no opportunity for a face-to-face meeting.
The urgency of the promptings of my inner being compelled me, in
any case, to explore with him my concerns about the faith of Ignatius
and my growing interest and eagerness to explore its underpinnings.
I imagined that upon his first reading of my missive, it would sting
as a splash of cold water on a morning face—taking his breath away
at first, and agitating him toward the one emptying the water bucket
in his direction. Still, I figured that after absorbing that initial shock
he would realize the sincerity of my inquiries and assist me in sorting
out my feelings, as he had always done with every challenge life had
raised for me. A part of me wished I had not sent the letter at all—the
thought of ripping it up had crossed my mind more than once as I
awaited the courier.

Weeks passed after I let it leave my hands, and my ambivalence in my conviction to send it did not abate. Thus, I did not venture toward Ignatius again, after the night I guarded him alone, for I feared being tempted by him further without the guidance of my father's words. When, and if, I spoke with him again, I told myself, I would likely do it with my father's blessings, by some form—if not enthusiasm, then with grudging permission—so that I might proceed in deeper discussions with Ignatius with the good heart of a faithful son.

Finally, weeks later, the courier arrived.

"Have you seen my father? Has he sent a response by you?" I asked.

"Yes, sir, Captain. He did indeed."

"Did he send me greetings?"

"Not in so many words, sir. He simply said, "Here. Take care to give this to my son, and swear to me that it will be for his eyes only. And, he gave me a special gratuity to make sure I sealed it so… But, sir, he looked uncheerful, not like when he sent messages by me to you at prior times. So, I reluctantly inquired of the soundness of his health."

"And said he in response…?"

"He turned no direct answer to me, Captain. He shrugged only, as one unsure of his words. It was not for me to inquire further, sir, as you know," he said quietly.

"I know. Thank you. Perhaps it is that his health is not prospering and he wishes to spare me worrying," I feigned in reply. Yet, I knew it was something different than that. My letter had cast him into a foul mood. How foul I did not know. But upon opening his letter and reading through it, my forecast of its contents was wildly mild, as his words struck me with a torrent of cascading condemnations.

Dear Aurelius, my son,

With great sorrow and crushing pain have I received your letter. I can scarcely breathe! Are you the Aurelius I reared? Whose life I planned? Who regarded me a man to be respected and followed in life and in death? Who, at a young age and later continuing, made me proud in my counsels with elders because of your precocious gifts to grasp, recite, and observe the essential traditions of Rome—most prominently including the demand of our state to honor the emperor and Roman deity? Who has received the favor of the gods in war and peace? Have not you?

Flummoxed and grieved am I beyond measure. Would that your words caused me to redden with anger, but, instead, I shrink in shame and disgust, shuddering to arrest the feeling both that I no longer know you and, more grievous still, that I no longer desire to. How could such evil thoughts harbor in your breast? How could you toy with atheist and atheism? Destruction? And the enemies of Rome? You flatter no one, least of all me, by wrapping your ridiculous new obsessions in the recall of the precious memories of your childhood, your upbringing, and your past loyalties to the gods and to me. I could, as now, feel no less futility about your life and my own, having lived it for you and Rome, than had I smothered the life out of you at birth. Should your present thoughts on this Ignatius and his superstition remain with you as you now say, would that I had done so, for, in any case, your life would have been no more lost.

Tell me now that your senses have returned! You have always been averse to acclaim, so tell me that you are confused by this man Ignatius's humility, mistaking that admirable quality in him for a pious subjugation to his pretend God, this Jesus, this Jesus Christ.

How can you, so well prepared and rooted in the finest of the traditions of Rome, prefer yesterday's god of Ignatius, soon to be forgotten, to the Roman gods of antiquity and immortality?

Surely this is momentary dithering brought on by your feelings that this Ignatius is a good man who does not deserve to die at the teeth of the lions! It can be nothing more than that, can it? I have never felt such a grave sense of estrangement from any person, any friend, as I now feel toward you, my own son, for I personally instructed you on the Roman way as you sat on my knees and slept in my house. I nurtured you with knowledge. I created you!

Thus, I have destroyed your letter so that none may ever read it and so that, upon your hoped-for change of heart, it will not condemn you or my name. I pray that it will not plunge my seed into ridicule and punishment, as growing out of our house, whose height may hereafter be measured only by the depths of absurdity to which it has fallen.

Be swift in your response and recantations to me, or be dead to me; dead to Rome. And dead to these preposterous, pernicious, and, yes, dangerous exchanges between us.

Claudius Maximus
Centurion of Rome, Retired

Staggered by my father's virulence, I fell to my knees, unable to speak or cry aloud. Inside, I groaned, "Oh, father, dear father. Father! I hoped not to lose you."

Tears flowed as when I, as a child, felt the strap of my father, administered without good cause. But these tears were of the bitter stripe. These tears were like those of one in mourning for the dead—and not just any dead but for a dead young friend, lost in war; as for a young child collaterally killed by a misplaced arrow or spear from his hand; as for the death of a devoted father, killed at the hand of a devoted son.

Never had my father used such vile and diabolical expressions. At most, I had expected strong words of caution and perhaps a warning of fear for my safety, should the Roman gods refuse their continued protection of me. And in my father's usual character, I expected him to engage me in a war of wits, cajoling me in repartees to pull me back into the fold—a fold I had not, at my writing to him, determined that I could leave. Certainly, I had imagined there would be follow-on letters, as my father attempted to guide me to a sound conclusion. However, a threatened—no, a guaranteed—bitter separation, with no ground for discussion, save complete recantation, giving no quarter to my sincere present search for an understanding of the supremacy of the spiritual powers of this world and the next, left me feeling empty and bewildered. Yes, my father could be stern and overbearing, strong-willed in giving me direction and instruction. Yet his stance in this response exposed him to me for the first time as selfish and shallow.

Suddenly, inexplicably, something sprang me out of my fog, bringing me to grips with the reality that my relationship with my father might be irretrievably lost. A part of me wanted to hurriedly write back and express sorrow at my musings about Jesus. Yet in that moment, I started to become persuaded that perhaps my father was right.

"The two of us are headed in different directions, embracing two hopelessly divergent perspectives—he to continue the unquestioned embrace of the gods of Rome and I drawn to search for the truth of the God Ignatius seeks to introduce to me."

The differences between these two choices, I knew in my heart, to be irreconcilable. "My father has made his choice. Now, it is left for me to make my own."

Oddly, my father's vitriol was breeding a new sense of freedom in me, a feeling of liberty to choose my way. The cloud of sadness draped over me lifted. Rising from my knees and wiping away my tears, I adjusted my garments, in the fashion of Ignatius, and, thinking on him, determined to seek him out, my heart skipping.

In the garden at midday, Ignatius sat speaking to some few peasants, it appeared, he chained to Publius and Dentatus, who were
ignoring him, talking among themselves.

"Ignatius, we travel in the direction of Troas tomorrow. Do you
feel fit to start out? Though I expect you are in no great hurry to reach
Rome, reach it we must. The months are passing and it is nearing
September, and the travel we must make by sea becomes treacherous
in the winter months. The emperor expects us there by the spring,
for a certain festival, where he wishes you to perform with his lions."

From whence these inappropriate comments originated, I could
not tell. It was if the evil one had control of my tongue, or more
properly, perhaps, I suddenly just felt the strange urge to look force-
ful and crude before my men to disguise my true interest in Ignatius.
The loud laughter from Publius and Dentatus affirmed that I had
gone too far on the side of tastelessness. Looking toward Ignatius,
I shook my head, slyly showing him my disappointment in myself.

Ignatius simply smiled.

"I have been praying for you," he said quietly. "Not the usual
prayer for you and your men since we started out, but praying for
you, only you."

I was speechless again, searching the eyes of the peasants and
those of my men, timorously, wondering if they thought I was in
secret league with Ignatius.

"I have prayed that you would open the door of your heart to
Jesus. He stands knocking for you. Can you not tell? He is seeking to
choose you, but first, you must open the door of your heart to Him."

"And how would you know that, old man? Have you heard His
voice from the clouds again?" I blurted out in defense.

"Audibly? No. But I know His sheep. He shows them to me in
my spirit, through His Spirit. You are destined to be one of them."

"Enough of this gibberish. We will travel tomorrow, whether
you like it or not. Publius, make sure all is ready. We leave at dawn,"
I said sternly. Yet, I was not convicted of my words. I was, in fact,
touched and made afraid by Ignatius's prophecy.

As I walked away, I could hear my men snickering and
murmuring.

"This Ignatius," Publius said, "he doesn't know Aurelius at all. I have seen him cut off the head of an enemy soldier, with him begging for mercy, and I have witnessed him leaving enemy prisoners to die in the snow. And Christians? Off with their heads," Publius declared, stomping toward Ignatius with his sword drawn to intimidate him.

Then, standing close to Ignatius, he sneered, "And I have seen Aurelius plunge his lance into the chests of men of your kind, so-called Christians, enemies of the state. He is no sheep. He is a wolf!"

Ignatius calmly replied to him, "In truth, he is neither. He is a leopard, as are you. A great hunter and a great killer. Not a wolf, for wolves run in packs, but he walks alone. Not yet a sheep is he either, but that will surely change."

"By Jupiter! You are a glorious fool, old priest," Publius announced, laughing heartily.

"Not by Jupiter will it be done, dear Publius," Ignatius intoned, happily, "but by Jesus!"

"Get up, Ignatius," Publius yelled. "It appears that the sun has fried your brains and old age has dimmed your vision."

And then he jerked Ignatius's chains, as Ignatius attempted to get his bearings to stand.

But Ignatius, still smiling at him, found his balance and did not fall down.

This would not be the last thing Ignatius would do that which would confound Publius on this trip to Rome.

CHAPTER 6
REVIVAL

"And it shall come to pass...that I will pour out my spirit upon all flesh...your old men shall dream dreams..."

—Joel 2:28 (KJV)

Ignatius visited the church in Philadelphia before our arrival in Smyrna. Large crowds met him there, including many church leaders. They engaged in lively discussions, more properly debates, over differences in what they called, "church doctrine," an unfamiliar term to me. At the conclusion of the meeting, Ignatius seemed morose, not flowing in his accustomed optimism. I therefore asked him whether the meeting had discouraged him.

"Sometimes," he said, "the man of God needs to be ministered to, and if not, then he must encourage himself until his spirit is quickened by the Holy Spirit. Sometimes he feels unready to lead his people, that he leaves work undone by leaving them too soon, and that he is unworthy of God's assignments. I felt all of these at certain points tonight. However, through my prayers and those of the church, of those of strong faith, my revival is at hand," he said kindly, "but thank you for asking about me."

Reading the letter he wrote to the Philadelphians disclosed how heavily these issues weighed on his heart. He wrote them:

> Do not err, my brethren, if anyone follow a schismatic, he will not inherit the Kingdom of God.

If any man walks about with strange doctrine, he cannot lie down in passion...for there is one Flesh of the Lord Jesus Christ, and one Cup in the union of His Blood; one altar.

My brethren, I am overflowing with love for you, and exceedingly joyful in watching over you. Yet, not I, but Christ; and in chains for His sake, I am more the fearful because I am not yet perfected. Your prayers, however, will make me perfect for God, so that I may win the lot which has so mercifully fallen to me...

I cried out while I was in your midst, I spoke with a loud voice, the voice of God: "give heed to the bishop and the presbytery and the deacons." Some suspected me of saying this because I had previous knowledge of the division which certain persons had caused; but He for whom I am in chains is my witness that I had no knowledge of this from any human being. It was the Spirit who kept preaching these words: "Do nothing without the bishop, keep your body as the temple of God, love unity, flee from divisions, be imitators of Christ, as He was imitator of the Father.

I did my best as a man devoted to unity. But, where there is division and anger, God does not dwell. The Lord, however, forgives all who repent, if their repentance leads to the unity of God... I have faith in the Grace of Jesus Christ; and He will remove from you every chain.

I beseech you, therefore...act according to Christian teaching. Indeed, I heard some men saying: "If I do not find it in the official records in the gospel, I do not believe." And, when I made answer to them, "It is written!" they replied, "That is not the point at issue." But, to me, the official record is Jesus Christ: the inviolable record is His cross, His death, and His resurrection, and the faith which He brings about: in these I desire to be justified by your prayers.

This letter I surmised he wrote on the way from Smyrna to Troas, because his secretary handed it to me on the evening of our arrival there. I only saw Ignatius briefly the following day, and he still appeared of a gloomy frame of mind. Though I thought to, I did not ask after him again, for I coldly told myself that I was not the keeper of his moods. Yet frankly, I believe I still stood somewhat wary of my strength to resist the draw of his message, should I stay in close contact with him.

On the morning after our second night in Troas, we suffered a great fright. Marius, who had been chained alone to Ignatius during the night, rapped furiously at my door, alarming me to outrageous thoughts of Christians attacking us, freeing Ignatius.

"Aurelius! Aurelius! An awful, tragic thing has struck, apparently in the night as we slept," Marius shouted out in a whisper as he came inside my room, closing the door behind him. "I have no idea what happened, but...but...!"

"Spit it out, Marius," I whispered back urgently. "Get a handle on yourself! Has Ignatius escaped?"

"Oh, I wish he had, Aurelius. Then, we might know what to do—to go after and recover him. But, sir, this... I don't know. I believe...it appears...he appears to be dead," he said, and his voice trailed off.

"Dead? Dead? By whose hand? How could this happen? Die he must, but, not in Troas. Was he poisoned? Did he take his own life?"

"I don't know. I don't even know if he is fully dead. It's, well... I cannot rouse him and his body's attitude is as stiff as a board. Come and see. Please, now. I have told no one else of this. Now, please!"

"Not fully dead? You make no sense, Marius!"

"Please, let's go, Aurelius!"

Gathering my clothes around me, my heart outracing my feet, in unparalleled anxiety I sped to Ignatius's holding place, as quietly as I could, so as not to wake all the others. There, on the floor of his room, he lay, out on his back, appearing to be in a lifeless, deep sleep. I put my ear to his chest to check his breathing and for heartbeats. His breathing barely registered, and his heartbeat was so faint that it was hardly detectable. I found his arms and legs rigid, as Marius had reported, but not yet cold, and, therefore, I believed, he was not yet dead.

"Ignatius! Ignatius!" I called out. "Wake up! Wake Up! Have you forgotten your promise to me to live until Rome? Wake up, I bid you! Are you gaming us? Is this some sorcerer's caper?"

Incoherent, I could not reason logically, and my questions felt foolish. Fear and remorse consumed me. I could only imagine the terrible wrath Trajan would unleash, should we lose Ignatius. Surely, he would have our heads. Short of that, he would drum us out of the army, with all of our decorations stripped. This, if our fellow soldiers did not laugh us out first, or our superiors push us out. Had I lacked foresight in not bringing a person with medical training along, given Ignatius's age and unhealthy look? Did I neglect my duty to him by allowing my men to abuse him, and by my own abuse of him? Should I have checked on him further to assess the dismal depths to which his constitution might have fallen? Mortified, I wallowed in self-pity and regret, worry bending my brow, and my hands, now cold, covering my face.

And then, a miracle. Suddenly, Ignatius sat straight up, as if a spring had thrust him forward, blinking at us, yawning and smiling, in good spirits.

"Good morning, men. God bless you! I've had a most splendid night!"

I'm sure he must have thought we'd glimpsed a ghost, for his face instantly showed perplexity as we recoiled from him as if he were a cobra, his cape flared, rising to strike.

"What on earth has you so fearful? Perhaps I should ask for a looking glass so that I may see myself as you see me. Quailing as you are before me, strong brave soldiers that you are, I may like my new look," Ignatius joked, surprisingly, obviously in a mood we had never observed in him.

"We thought you were…"

"Dead? Oh, I see, then. I can assure you I was not. And, having not died, I am not resurrected from the dead. I know you Romans see a god in every cloud and conversation, so you may know, Aurelius, I am not one of them," Ignatius continued, joking, seeming to me a little sarcastic.

His light attitude and misguided humorous attempts, after our heart-stopping fright, angered us.

"You are having far too much fun at our cost," I offered calmly, though I wanted to shout at him. I showed caution, for though I hated Ignatius's teasing, my gratefulness at his recovery, and my hope that he would not relapse into another episode of sleeping stiffly and breathing in small sips, restrained me.

"What happened to you?" Marius joined in, still a little shaken. "How did you manage to do that? Holding your breath still and your body stiff?"

"I fell into a trance. I had no control over it. Had I, I would not have left it, for in it I dreamt the most marvelous dream and set my eyes upon visions so wondrous as not to appear in this world," Ignatius said, looking upward and opening his arms wide.

"I was a little child again. And I beheld the face and touch of Jesus as before—all those years before. Marvelous. So blessed. Thank you, Jesus! Thank You, Jesus," he extolled.

"Whatever are you babbling, Ignatius? Isn't it enough that you know this magic, how to use enchantments to enthrall and scare us? Why must you use it to convict us of the craftiness of your God as well?" Marius asked impatiently.

"You speak foolishly, Marius," Ignatius responded, angrily. "Stop taunting God before, in your ignorance, you curse yourselves and your posterity. I did nothing. Jesus did everything. It was amazing!"

Ignatius spoke so chillingly and authoritatively that it immediately set Marius and me to shuddering, feeling fear now of a different kind— the fear of his powerful God. We looked upon Ignatius with awe.

"Tell us what you saw in your…your trance," Marius said somberly. I nodded agreement.

A smile creased Ignatius's wrinkled face again as his eyes rolled heavenward in pleasant reflection.

"I was a child, among many other children, gathered around Jesus. He blessed us and spoke softly, warmly, to each of us, touching the crowns of our heads. My face glowed with his touch, and I felt so light that my feet left the ground. I was...I was unspeakably happy. I cannot otherwise explain it."

"What did He say to you?" I asked.

"Jesus said, 'You are my child. Never will I leave you. Whither you go, I will go.'

Then, he repeated it over and over until I could not be still in His presence as joy overcame me and I ran leaping, as a young antelope, dancing before its mother. My happiness, oh, my happiness. Unimaginable!"

He continued, "It was far greater than when he touched me before, when I was a child near four years old. This time he touched me as His child, not merely as a child. Though I now have the wisdom of my years, yet I received His touch this time as a little child, innocent in heart, surrendered to Him without reserve, trusting Him completely, as a child trusts His earthly father.

"And, a field of flowers, more gorgeous than any I have ever seen, surrounded Him and us. His face, shining like the sun, His majesty, compelling a thousand-fold more than that of Trajan, His look and His touch, most affectionate. He sat on a bench made of braided flowers as he greeted us. Angels sang above us, echoing His greetings, then they called us to them, and we ran into their arms, and they lifted us aloft, as my father used to lift me in play. We laughed and sang with them. We sang songs of praise to Jesus and of thanksgiving. I cannot now repeat the words of the songs, for they are beyond my capacity to do so, except that the sounds thereof were incomparably euphonious. It was paradise."

Amazed, vicariously Marius and I became caught up in the experience Ignatius described. Our hearts began to feel his joy. And like him, we did not wish that sensation to end.

"How can we see Jesus?" I asked. "Can we see Him as you have?"

"You can see Him, but in your own way and through your own gifts, the gifts that He gives to you, to each of us. You simply have to ask Him to see Him, and, He will answer you, with the answer that is right for you."

Marius and I stood transfixed by Ignatius's words. Seeing our rapt interest, Ignatius pressed on, further describing his seraphic experience.

"I saw something more in my dream. I saw many men, men drawn to Christ, men building his church, men from all over the Earth, in numbers like the grains of sand. And a voice declared that this had happened because other men sacrificed, became living and loving sacrifices. Some of these men were of our times, others from times in the future. But then I knew, more than before, that God appointed me to my present mission, to be a sacrifice for His cause before men, confidently and steadfastly drawing men to Him, through showing them the power of love, of the love of Christ. I am…I am…completely satisfied. Completely."

Recalling my own dream, in which I incredibly became a follower of Jesus, the words burst forth from my mouth without my realizing I spoke them.

"Did you see me? Did you see Marius or me among their faces?"

"I could not see the face of any man. There were many colors, and the faces shone in a kaleidoscope. A number of them wore the colors of the army of Rome. Perchance you could be numbered among those in the future. But they were all changed, celestially changed in glory. I did not see my face there, but I know that it was there…"

"Roman soldiers?" Marius asked, anxiously.

"Yes. Roman soldiers. But they were no longer soldiers for Rome, nor for the emperor, but soldiers of Almighty God, the King of kings. They and all of them marched in an incomparable procession—but a procession not led by armies or centurions, nor by emperors or kings, but by little children."

And then, incomprehensibly, Marius and I feel to our knees before Ignatius, with the same mind. We seemed to say these words in unison:

"Pray for us. Pray for us, Ignatius. Pray that we may have your faith and your wisdom; your joy and your peace."

"Pray," I added, "not just for Marius and me but for all of my men."

So this morning, I prayed and Marius prayed to the God of Ignatius for the first time. We did not know what to say. We just followed Ignatius as he tugged us forward. It would not be the last time that he or we would do so.

A day later, Ignatius sent a letter back to the church at Smyrna. No longer agape at him, but feeling a genuine oneness with him, I looked forward to reading that letter, not for any signs of treason, as before, for I knew evil could find no quarter in him, but rather to confirm my hope that his optimism had been fully restored. Given the ecstasy that engulfed him, Marius, and me the previous night, I knew that it had.

He wrote to the Smyrnaeans:

> I give glory to Jesus Christ, the God who made you wise, for I have observed that you are set in unshakeable faith, as if nailed to the cross of our Lord, Jesus Christ in body and soul; that you are confirmed in love by the Blood of Christ.
>
> He underwent all sufferings for us, so that we might be saved... When they say that His passion was merely in appearance; it is they who exist only in appearance; and as their notion, so shall it happen to them. They will be bodiless and ghostlike shapes. I know and believe that He was flesh after the resurrection. And, when He came to see Peter, He said to them; "Here, now, touch Me, and see that I am not a bodiless ghost." Immediately they touched Him and, because of the merging of His flesh and spirit, they believed. For the same reason they despised death and in fact were proven superior to death. If it were merely in appearance that these things were done by our Lord, then it is merely in appearance that I am a prisoner.
>
> Take note of those who hold heterodox opinions on the grace of Jesus Christ which have

come to us, and see how contrary their opinions are to the mind of God. For love, they have no care, not for the widow, not for the orphan, not for the distressed, not for those in prison or freed from prison, nor for the hungry and thirsty. They are…perishing in their disputes. It would be better for them to have love, so that they might rise again…

I, Aurelius, rejoiced in my own spirit. I rejoiced because I knew that the revival in Ignatius's spirit for which he prayed had broken out. I knew that our prayers, those of his churches, and the supernatural force of his dreams had now visited him, quickening his spirit and lingering with him, but also falling on us.

CHAPTER 7
DEVIL IN THE DETAILS

"No man also having drunk old wine, straightway
desireth new; for he saith, The old is better."
—Luke 5:39 (KJV)

Several nights ago, when Ignatius prayed together with Marius and me and shared his incredible dream with us, I felt certain that I met Jesus. I felt certain that I believed in Him and that I wanted to give my life serving and trusting Him. Still, in these few days since, melancholy feelings have threatened to take hold in me.

"Don't feel dejected with yourself or that you are weak," Ignatius counseled me. "Jesus will train you up slowly, gradually, to his disciplines. He is patient with you, to learn His ways. You must, therefore, be patient with yourself. As you become acclimated to listening to His Holy Spirit and letting it guide you, you will abound in your new faith. But also remember, Jesus is a Spirit, now in your spirit, you having become a spirit being yourself. In the spirit world are evil forces that will war against you holding on to your new conviction. Pray to Him that you may resist them."

Therefore, I prayed that the Holy Spirit would help me fight against all forces, in the Earth or any other world, that would pull me away from faith in Him, and my conviction in Him strengthened day by day, as did that of Marius, who daily prayed with me.

All our lives, we had diligently followed the faiths of our fathers—in their gods and traditions and in their belief in imperial deities. Yet there could be no place for such beliefs as we embraced

Christianity. None of what I now understood Christianity to be necessarily involved signs and wonders, as I first thought, but love for God and men based on and because of His redemption of men from sin. The "nightmare" that had caused me such consternation—the vision in which I saw myself as "one of them," a Christian, I reflect on now as the most wonderful of dreams. Feeling Jesus present with me, walking with me and me with Him, opened me to desire to know Him better and better. Ignatius was not hasty with us in his instruction, and not disappointed in our questions, no matter how immature. We relished our new training and inspiration, which Ignatius now said was our new "calling," to serve Jesus.

Our old ways tempted us, especially as we went about our duties with my men. Yet, so excited were Marius and I about our emergent experiences with Jesus through Ignatius that we burst with eagerness to share it with my men. Recalling my own father's severe rebuke of me for merely inquiring about Christianity, I, more than Marius, dreaded my men's reactions. Yet for some reason, we didn't want to hold that news inside of us alone.

"I cannot tell you how you should do this thing that you wish to do with your comrades, but I can say this. Having confessed your belief in Jesus Christ to me, and more importantly to Him, you are obligated to witness to His truth. For He has said in His Word that He will not own those who say they accept Him but do not own Him openly. Every Christian is called to witness to the truth of Christ. The timing and the methodology you use in doing this may be of your choosing, but do it you must," Ignatius answered us when we put the question to him.

Discussing the matter between us, we knew that Ignatius was right, both because of the justifications he offered and because we knew that our colleagues were growing suspicious of our interactions with Ignatius. They could also see that things had changed between Ignatius and me. I showed Ignatius new kindnesses. At first, I commanded that he no longer be chained in leg irons as he slept or rested. Then, I ordered that all restraints be removed and that he be permitted to sleep alone, without guards inside his room at night, but rather posted outside at his door. Grumbling at these changes ensued, led mostly by Publius. To keep things in good order, I knew I had to assert myself as captain, as a man of integrity, and for the first time, unbelievably, as a Christian. I told Marius that I would speak only for myself, leaving him to reveal his position on Christianity at another time or not at all, as he decided. He turned no answer to me, but seemed in deep contemplation, so I did not further disturb him about it.

I gathered my men together to bare my soul.

"Please, tell us why we are all here. It is late and no one watches our prisoner," Publius began, moments after I called the meeting to order, preemptively attempting to take it over.

"Bishop Ignatius hardly presents a risk of escape, Publius. His room is locked and his windows barred, besides. But I tell you that if we all decided to abandon our mission, return to Syria, and leave Ignatius here alone, I believe that he would secure his own passage to Rome to keep his appointment with the emperor's lions."

At this, my men interrupted me with laughter, for after six months of traveling with Ignatius, they all knew that I had spoken the truth.

"So, my dear Publius, let the threat of Ignatius's escape be the least source of our worry tonight," I concluded, reveling in the support of my men. "By all events, I do not expect that we will meet very long. I want to inform you of a transformative event in my life that you should hear about from me—that I very much want to tell you about."

I spoke boldly, but my throat was dry. I said a silent prayer, asking the Holy Spirit to settle me so that I might speak with authority for Jesus. Immediately, I felt my spirit rest.

"We are charged with the mission, under the orders of Emperor Trajan, to deliver Ignatius to Rome for execution. Nothing will deter me or us in that responsibility. As your captain, as leader of this troop, I will support each of you in what you need in order to do your part in getting that job done. What I say here and now is totally separate—has absolutely nothing to do with the fulfillment of the mission to which we are assigned.

"I cannot know for certain why Emperor Trajan imposed the sentence on Ignatius that he did. It was not simply because he is a

Christian. For all these other Christians we have encountered on this journey and those of whom we know in our local areas are not so sentenced. Trajan does not order them chained to soldiers and escorted to Rome to be cast into a den of lions. They operate freely within the Empire. Their presence is tolerated, unless they are shown to be, upon a proper charge, involved in acts of sedition against our state, and they then are then appropriately punished.

Present at his sentencing, I believe that a principal reason for Ignatius's sentence was the insolence he displayed before the emperor. He drew Trajan's attention to him, and to me, along Trajan's parade route in Antioch, Ignatius and his band of Christian followers glaring contemptuously at Trajan. Absent that inappropriate display, he would never have been dragged to Trajan's palace to face his ire, and ultimately, his condemnation. No man may disrespect our emperor and live. That is the law of the realm, and will be, so long as the State of Rome exists, which we all trust and believe will be forever.

Having said that, I must confess to you that Bishop Ignatius's teachings have affected me mightily. His words have stirred my spirit. His displays of love and forgiveness so changed my view of him and so intrigued me that I longed to know what motivated this character in him. Thus, I inquired, I listened, I learned from him about the God he serves. I have shared with you the letters he wrote to churches along the way. Can any of you say that there is anything seditious or harmful to Rome in them? In that regard, their messages are benign. But in another sense, his letters express transcendent messages, and I confess to you I now believe, transcendent truths about the love of his God toward men, and His sovereignty over men and over the other gods that men worship. My friends, soldiers of the State of Rome to which we have all devoted our lives, I must confess to you honestly—I believe in Ignatius's teachings. His demonstrated commitment to Jesus by his words and his actions further convict me that a special supreme authority governs his life. I believe in his God. I have…I have adopted his God as my God. I continue also to believe in Rome, to which I have sworn allegiance, including my allegiance to give my life in its defense. In my belief in Jesus Christ as my resurrected Savior and in Rome as the state of my whole-hearted allegiance, I see no inconsistency. This is not an easy conversation, but it is one I felt I must have with you. I…"

Publius angrily interrupted me.

"I suspected as much, Aurelius. All your secret meetings at strange hours, all your long talks with this criminal. Your contrivance of sweet and soothing words to mollify us in the face of your scandalous announcement of belief in Jesus is transparent and shows weakness in your constitution. How can you say that you can bear allegiance to Rome and this… Jesus at the same time, without injury to either? What of the immortal gods of Rome? Are they now, in your heart and mind, subservient to this Jesus, or do they exist to you anymore at all?"

I swallowed hard, sweat accumulating on my brow. I stared into the cold eyes of Publius.

Publius was as decorated a soldier as was I, and a rival in leadership in the Roman Army, and now, it appeared, in my own present troop. The emperor had chosen me to secure his person in a large swath of Central Asia Minor, and that of his forts and cities there, over Publius, who had vied for that position. Otherwise, we held the same rank in the army and appeared to enjoy the chance for equally high trajectories to the upper ranks over the span of our careers. Nearly the same age, we were equally fearless in battle and had the respect of all who fought alongside us. Presently, though, I enjoyed more favor with Trajan, largely because of the brilliant service my father had rendered to Trajan in past military expeditions. Publius sorely envied that. However, through my own service and sacrifice, I had earned my emperor's respect, trust, and devotion. Publius's present challenge to me, baring his teeth so menacingly at me before my men, showed me that Publius would seize on my confession of faith to drive an impenetrable and immovable wedge between me and the emperor, with Publius positioning himself to paint me as far less loyal to Trajan than was he.

I had fretted over whether to include Publius in my troop, whose members, under Trajan's order, I solely picked. I had, however, truly feared that the passage from Syria to Rome would be fraught with dangerous designs by Ignatius's supporters to free him, and had therefore reasoned that I needed the stoutest men possible under my command. Publius certainly fit that requirement. I could not have anticipated Ignatius's zeal to die for the cause of Christ, the lack of fear that he and other Christians had of death, and thus the lack of any interest or motivation on their parts to rescue him from his sentence of death—at least not through the force of arms. Had I had the foresight of these things, I would never have included Publius, for I knew of his difficult personality and ambitions. Yet how could I have known such things about Christians, with whom I had had no association, except to round up any of them charged with sedition, and then seeing them only at the tip of my lance or my gladius?

At this pressurized moment, I blamed myself for not knowing more of the true security risk the trip to Rome involved, because I counted myself a careful planner and hard thinker. And too, at this moment, in my infancy as a Christian, I found myself blaming Jesus Christ for my predicament. Then I heard the words of Ignatius: "Pray. Ask the Holy Spirit to help you!" I bowed my head, prayed, and found my response.

"Publius, before you judge my sincerity, answer me this. Do you find Ignatius a plotter against Rome, though he be a Christian? Do you find that Ignatius expresses love for Emperor Trajan, even for us, Trajan's loyal soldiers and Ignatius's tormentors, though he be a Christian? How, then, can you question whether I can be and am both loyal to Rome, even more than Ignatius, and yet a Christian even with him?

That question confounded Publius and surprised me, for I knew that I was not a man of such words and that the wisdom they contained, flowing from my mouth, did not originate in my mind. Publius did not answer, as he sat pondering how to deal with my deep retort. The men, however divided in opinion over my announcing myself a Christian, seemed to be as one in thinking Publius's attack against me too severe, inconsiderate, and, given our respective stations, bordering on insubordination. Some wanted to hear me out. All thought that I should be heard out.

"May I speak, Aurelius?" Dentatus asked respectfully.

"Of course. Please. And, anyone else who would like to do so."

"I, too, have been puzzled by Ignatius and, I admit, impressed by his character—his gentleness, his concern for the welfare of others, even expressing love for his enemies. However, we are men of tradition. We are men of Rome, and in Rome there is but one way things are done. We honor the gods of our fathers because they do, and this we never question. In fact, given that Rome succeeds like no other nation on Earth, we believe under the protection of these gods, we have seen no need to shop for other gods, and certainly not one to replace all those of our traditions. If Ignatius's admittedly admirable character and integrity is the product of his god working in his life, of the god he serves, then that is a powerful reason for him to observe and honor him. But for we who are accustomed to the old ways of the Empire when it comes to religion, why should we seek, let alone adopt, the new ways presented to us by Ignatius?"

"My dear Dentatus," I responded, "you have inquired incisively. Thank you. Feeling that I would fail my father kept my soul's aching for new knowledge of Jesus captive, locked away under his arrest. My father is my example of the finest in soldiering and manhood, a well-deserved example. I still desire that he will find it within his being to approve of my decision, for it pains me that we should suffer any estrangement. But when I try the gods of my father for myself, when I speak to them, I hear not even echoes of my own words in return. My appeals to them are as if to the dead, the lifeless. And when I make sacrifices to them, pour perfume and wine at their feet, I am left with only empty ewers and spots on my floor and rugs to remove and make clean. But when I pray to Jesus, I know from deep inside He stirs me, and I can hear and feel love and assurance, which cleanses me. I feel power and peace. I feel protected and fearless. I know that He is more than plaster or wood, more than copper or brass, more than a stone or an earthen statue. He lives in me and breathes on me, and is the great Sovereign of my life. He is a Spirit, not created by the imaginations of philosophers but existing by His own unction. It is He who has imagined and created this world and all that is in it. But to experience Him, to know Him as I do, you must have the courage to test tradition and to invite Him into your heart, to give Him authority over your life."

These words, too, I knew, as soon as they left my lips, were beyond my comprehension or ability to articulate. They were like the words of Ignatius, spoken through me, and authentically the ones I needed to say to reach out to my men, to prod them to search their hearts and to understand and accept the sincerity of my own.

"You say that if one asks to have such a thing—such a truth—revealed to him, that it will happen?" Otho inquired, intrigued.

"It is not magic, that happens with the flip of a coin or a flash of light, but, yes, it will happen for you, if you sincerely seek to know Him."

My confidence soared, now unbendable. All trepidation departed me, and an eagerness to share all with my men engulfed me. I poured more and more out of my heart over them in answer to their questions. Most of them intently engaged with me.

However, seeing the tables tipping from the initial shock he saw on the faces of the men at the instance of my announcement to them, to the various looks presently on their faces of agreement, curiosity, engagement, and understanding, Publius, unconvinced and unwilling to let me carry the day, figuratively thrust his lance into my chest.

"Do you contend, dear Aurelius, that this Jesus is greater than our Divine Emperor Trajan?"

I had danced around this issue from the start of tonight's meeting. Though it was true that Ignatius was sentenced to die because of insolence, for showing a lack of respect before the face of Trajan and the institutions of the Empire and for failing to cheer him at his parade, I suspected that his life still might have been spared, had he answered Crassus's question about the deity of Trajan affirmatively. Though I had answered truthfully—that I believed that the State of Rome and faith in Christ could indisputably co-exist, I had not addressed the matter of Trajan's deity, or whether Trajan must be subjugated to Jesus Christ, a position I now believed to be the lot of every man. Feeling an ebbing in my once-surging confidence, I prayed that the Holy Spirit would give me wisdom to respond as He would have me do, just as Ignatius had instructed me. Before I could respond, however, the voice of my friend pierced the air.

"I do. I, indeed, do," Marius spoke up, his voice cracking as in tears. "Caesar was not a god. No one declared him to be so while he lived. Yet Emperor Augustus and Emperor Trajan are? How can that be? Either all emperors are gods or none of them are. Honorable men are they all. Deserving of our allegiance, loyalty, and respect? Without question. Worthy to follow into battle and to risk our lives, even give our lives, in their causes? Doubtless. But able to rescue us from the state of that death to an eternal after-life, not lost in the shadows of this world but in the light of the firmament, in resplendent, sublime glory, in perfect happiness? No! And no emperor has ever made such a claim, indeed, no god of Rome ever has. Should we not wish this, though, for all Rome? Should we not wish this for our beloved emperor?"

My heart burst with joy and admiration for my friend.

"I join with Marius in what he has spoken," I added quietly, saying all that needed to be said. So complete were Marius's remarks that I could, immediately, think of nothing to add.

Yet after a brief moment of reflection, I said, "The God of Ignatius is the God of the universe, in control of all things, available to help ensure the continued vitality of Rome and all that are within it."

Publius, beside himself in outrage, shouted, "Are these words not blasphemy? Are they not words unworthy of the leader of this troop to Rome? Are we so weakly led as to be taken in by an old soothsayer, this filthy rag of a man and his invisible god? Would that I had never joined this sorry troop! Would that I had never called you friend, Aurelius, and you, Marius! You are traitors to Rome!"

Arising from my seat, I lunged toward Publius, for my love of Rome ran deep, to my bones, and I dared any man to question me in that regard. Not retreating, Publius moved forward to engage me, and I advanced toward him. However, my men stepped in, holding us back from a physical confrontation.

"You are a fool, Publius!" I told him. "Would that I had left you in Syria. Your ambition darkens your heart, now as always. The charge of this troop is given to me by Emperor Trajan, and I will permit only him to relieve me of it. You are a soldier under my command and you are dangerously close to feeling the entirety of the brunt of my superiority over you. Any other acts as you have pulled tonight will be dealt with harshly, and finally, under the conditions of Roman law that pertain for one who rebels in the field of battle against his commander."

"Be that as it may, Aurelius. Perhaps the emperor, hearing of your conversion, will reconsider his appointment of you to this responsibility. Perhaps it will be my duty to inform him."

"Do with that as your conscience dictates, Publius. He will not believe you, for he knows that while you are a brave man, your judgment is often suspect. He will require that he hear from me personally and thoroughly on any complaint made against me by you. To complete this mission, I need not advise him that I believe in the reality of the God of Ignatius. By delivering Ignatius to his death in the Roman Coliseum, I will thereby prove my loyalty to him and to the purposes to which he assigned my hands. You will not abandon your duty to him and to Rome by failing to see this mission through under my command, despite all of your newfound doubts in my leadership. Hear me well. I will have you shackled or have you fall under my sword before I again tolerate you ever calling me a traitor to Rome or to Emperor Trajan. That is all, Publius! You are dismissed!"

At that, Publius walked out of the meeting, as did several others of my men. Those who remained wanted to hear more, learn more about Jesus. They were not yet convinced that He was who Marius and I said he was. So, some sat with us and with Ignatius from day to day. In doing so, they sought to test their reluctance to abandon the old for the new—paganism for Christianity, traditions for grace, shadows for substance. They sought to taste new wine.

But Publius, the devil possessing him, seethed and plotted against us, and especially against me, hoping to ensure, that though these men might smell the aroma, perhaps even sip the new wine that Ignatius and I were offering them, they would not grow to become new winebibbers.

CHAPTER 8
SOUR GRAPES NO MORE

"In those days they shall say no more, the fathers have eaten a sour grape, and the children's teeth are set on edge."
—*Jeremiah 31:29 (KJV)*

Regulus rode hard for almost two days straight, covering nearly fifty miles. A letter received from his son, Marius, prompted him to rush to see his friend and former commander, Claudius, the father of Aurelius. He and Claudius served in the Legio X Fretensis, stationed in Jerusalem but responsible to cover most of the military requirements of Central Asia Minor. Claudius was no ordinary century but a senior century, a Primus Pilus, with nearly one thousand men under his command at the height of his service. Regulus had had the honor of serving as his Optiones, the second in command of the Tenth Century.

Regulus and Claudius fought together in many battles, including the first Jewish-Roman War, and the siege of Masada with Emperor Trajan. Claudius, a very hard man in the training and discipline of his men, wielded his "vitis," or vine staff, mercilessly, earning him a reputation as a brutal commander. His men followed him because he just as brutally crushed all enemies in his path, leading and inspiring his men by example. So overwhelming was his skill and courage that no man under his command doubted that he'd earned and deserved his rank. Yet Claudius's harsh actions more than once engendered mutinous thoughts on the part of a few of his soldiers. Indeed, after he had broken his vine staff over the back of one soldier, that soldier had attempted to kill him. It had been Regular's lot, then, to watch Claudius's back, and to also attempt, when he could find Claudius in the mood to receive it, to urge Claudius to moderate his punishment and overly hard disciplining of his men. Regulus had saved Claudius from both his men and himself several times over their careers, and he was on a mission to do something on that order again this morning. As the hoofbeats of his horse lost the sounds of grass and dirt thumping beneath them and took on the clopping sounds of hooves against stones, in the morning light he could see the large gate at the end of the wide stone road leading into Claudius's country estate. He stopped about ten feet from the impressive gate, gazing upon it. The gate bore the Legio X Fretentsis's name and symbols: the bull, Taurus, the holy animal of the goddess Venus; a ship, for "Fretensis" meant "of the sea strait," depicting, on the ship's sides, the battles of Naulochus and Actium, won before their times; and the familiar boar, the holy animal representing the god of the sea, Neptune. Regulus smiled within himself at the memories these symbols evoked. But, then, he silently winced at the thought of having to deal with Claudius over them on this, his self-imposed assignment. He let out a loud sigh, reflexively, at this daunting prospect, abruptly waking the slave napping at the gate.

"Who goes there?" the humongous, startled slave snorted. "Announce yourself, so that I may inform the master who sits so noisily at his gate."

Regulus laughed at the formality of the slave. His old friend truly had retired to luxurious living, as he had been told. And, from the looks of things, he'd made the adjustment from hard-charging soldier to country gentleman quite successfully.

"Tell him an old friend is here. Just say his Optiones, Regulus, stands noisily at his gate."

"Tell him his what?"

"Just say Regulus. He'll know."

Gone for just a minute, the old slave returned beaming. "He asked me to show you in right away, and told me to excuse your noise."

"Tell him...oh, forget that. Why am I sending messages through you? Open the gate," Regulus said, laughing.

Regulus spotted a man whom he thought to be Claudius, but he was much bigger than the Claudius he'd known eight years earlier, when he'd last seen him. Still, his voice was unmistakable.

"Regulus? It is you? Come on in, old friend! Take his horse, Clius. By Mercury, you rode him hard. He is lathered all over. I am surprised he didn't drop under you. Given the look of your steed, I am tempted to look over your shoulder to see if the enemy chased you here. But my goodness, it is great to see you. Later I will show you around the place. But, now, tell me what brings you here in such a rush?"

Claudius put his arm around Regulus's shoulder and continued joking with him. He whispered: "If the emperor has sent you here to recruit me to join in some military campaign, you look as if you are up to it, but tell him that, with respect, I am too old, too fat, and too retired to be of use to him. Anyway, for a man of your years to ride through the night to see me, it must be very important. I would hope you are using your retirement years to rest and keep what strength remains in you and not taking up new causes."

Claudius gabbed on, egging Regulus to spit things out. But Regulus, as in the old days, knew he had to pick his spot to talk over what he'd come to discuss.

"Well, I will. But get me inside your home first. Greet me properly and I may get around to telling you of the mission I'm on."

Claudius had indeed grown fat, his big belly rising and heaving under his tunic as he laughed. Regulus felt the hard rolls around his midriff as they walked, half hugging each other, through the portals of the house. They paused at the entrance to pay homage at the shrine of Lares, with its bright bronze statuettes dancing in gay poses. They acknowledged Janus there too, the god of the doorway. Finally, they bowed to a large statute of Vesta, goddess of the hearth. Seeing all these gods, Regulus became more keenly aware of the magnitude of the challenge that lay ahead around the discussion of the new faith of Marius and Aurelius that he'd come to have with Claudius.

"How have you been, dear friend?" Regulus began, diplomatically. "I can see from the look of you and this place that your barns are full of wheat and barley, your vineyards saturated with ripened grapes, your wine vats overflowing, and your animals well fed. The signs of prosperity abound."

"Stop with the attempt at flattery, Regulus. I've let myself go, quite deliberately. Forty years I spent in the service of Rome. I wanted to make sure that when I retired, I would never be reenlisted in service to the army. Who recalls an old soldier whose walk has turned into a waddle and whose once-iron belly is more a sudsy tub than a steel drum?"

"Now, you may be accused of pulling the wool. Your most important skill, as we both know, resides in your mind, not in your muscles, no matter how atrophied you claim them to be. The brightness of your eyes and your wit betray the suggestion that your mind is disabled to any degree by your girth. No one knew the strategies of warfare like you. So, you may have let yourself grow fat for nothing. Besides, the Empire is at relative peace."

To this they both laughed, raising their goblets of red wine and greedily recalling old war stories.

"Have another, Regulus," Claudius urged, after two goblets had been downed by each of them. I don't expect any more visitors this morning. If I do, I will have my giant slave growl at them and run them off. I have not had this delightful a visit in a long time, and, besides, I need a good excuse for this early-morning wine indulgence."

Though Claudius had been Regulus's commander, they had much in common that leveled out their relationship and created bonds, making them trusted friends. Their sons, Marius and Aurelius, were the same age and had grown up, from small boys, to be best friends. This caused their paths to intersect as they dealt with the common issues between them of raising high-spirited boys of busy and ambitious fathers. They chose the same trainers for their sons, eager to make them ready for careers in the Roman Army, to follow in their footsteps. Furthermore, each suffered through the loss of his wife, their wives dying of diseases a few years apart, leaving Claudius and Regulus to work through and lean on each other through the seemingly impossible task, starting out, of being both father and mother to their sons. They survived it all, raising two fine sons who had become highly successful soldiers. Importantly, they had also trained their sons in common regarding religion, teaching them to identify and appreciate the close ties between civic and military affairs on the one hand and religious observances on the other. In Rome, the household and not the individual was the unit of society in all aspects of domestic life—including religion. And the responsibility for every aspect of life, especially of the household, fell primarily on the head of the family, the father, "pater familias," who acted on behalf of it. Religious observances of Rome, "sacra privata," were binding on him as the family's head. An inheritance that did not include passing on these things to a father's posterity was worthless.

"Oh, no, no," Regulus protested, holding up his hands to prevent the slave girl from pouring a third cup of wine. "Maybe later, if I am permitted to stay for the evening meal. No need for me to grow accustomed to mornings of fine wine, unless I am to take up a high-paying retirement job, perhaps as a lictor, to supplement my retirement pay."

"A lictor? You? Going around with some senator or magistrate and flogging and beheading poor souls unfortunate enough to offend one of these puffed-up persons? Not you. That would not be a job for you. But me? I could stomach it," he said, laughing merrily and patting his enormous gut. "But I wouldn't, even for the highest price. Looking back, I've seen enough bloodshed, on the battlefield and on the streets. My togas and tunics have been free of bloodstains for some years now, and I plan to keep them that way."

Feeling that he had reached a point with Claudius where his mood was sufficiently relaxed, Regulus carefully opened the subject that he'd come to talk over.

"I've hastened to see you, my dear friend, because of our sons," he began, speaking softly, looking Claudius in the eyes.

Immediately, the gay expression left Claudius's face, making it clear that the subject was unwelcome.

"We must talk about them," Regulus pressed. "I cannot share the news I have received from Marius with anyone in the world except you, for I am too ashamed. They both…both of our boys seem to hold the same view on this…this Christianity, and I figured, if we put our minds together, we could figure…"

Claudius looked hard at Regulus, anger glinting in his eyes.

Regulus hurried to continue.

"I don't understand them. I am hoping that you could…that you could help me or that…perhaps we could help each other. Well, I don't know, really. I'm at my wits' end, and I felt sure you would know what to do. You always have," Regulus said, his voice trailing off, his confidence sagging.

"How did you learn about Aurelius?" Claudius interjected abruptly, angrily. "I hope Marius informed you secretly, so that this thing is not spread."

"Marius sent his letters directly to me by a paid messenger. I think it arrived discreetly," Regulus, said with restraint, surprised at Claudius's seeming attack.

Seeing the disappointment in Regulus's eyes, Claudius caught himself.

"Forgive me, Regulus. I wondered… I've heard rumblings from one quarter about Aurelius and religion, some mocking references I am told. I wondered how it was spreading. You're my friend, and I did not mean to accuse you, a welcome guest in my house. I…look. We're both struggling with this. I know that. You would have nothing to profit from letters getting out about our sons' indiscretions, from these unfortunate leanings breaking containment. Yet I suspect they have enemies in their ranks—men who feel as betrayed as do we… Well, I should speak for myself. Times were that I could speak for my entire household. But it appears, with Aurelius's maverick streak springing free, no longer can I say that, even for my own son. I used to admire his free spirit. Now I wish I had broken him. Oh, Regulus! I feel deeply betrayed. Were I led by such a man as Aurelius has shown himself to be, I would be tempted to pray to the gods for the strength to remove him from his command by force…by force! By force, as some tried to do to me for other reasons. That is why I am worried. Though I have lost Aurelius as a son, I am trying to stay away from desiring to see him found with a dagger in his back by the hand of one of his disgruntled men."

"I know, Claudius. I'm afraid that danger is real. This is my principal reason for rushing to see you. Listen to this part of Marius's letter." Regulus retrieved the letter, which he had securely fastened within a pouch tied inside of his toga.

He read: "Publius is not like the others of our men. Most of them do not understand all that Aurelius and I are experiencing, but they are trying to. They, by all events, believe that Aurelius remains true to his oath and mission to Rome, despite his growing strange questions about religion. There are four others who wholly agree with Publius, though not as angrily. But Publius requires constant watching. I don't fear for my life, nor Aurelius for his. But it is more my duty to guard his back, both because he is really the object of Publius's hate and because I see it as my responsibility to protect my captain and my friend. Sending word to you of my new faith and his, and my new worries about Aurelius, is not to add vexation to your life. I pray that the God I now serve will give you peace and a heart open to understanding. I have prayed to Him for you to that end."

Stony silence followed. Regulus tried to break it with a spark of cheeriness to restore talkativeness to Claudius.

"It looks as if my son is playing the same role for Aurelius, in saving his backside, as I did for you," he cautiously jested.

But that did not touch Claudius. He arose and turned his back to Regulus, fighting back tears.

"I no longer have a son," he mumbled, "nor do I want to know him or help him do what he is doing. He disowns the most essential lessons in Roman life that I carefully taught him. He has dishonored the gods of my father and his own. No good will befall him. He is lost, Regulus, hopelessly, irretrievably lost. Perhaps…and these are words I thought I could never even think, let alone say…but perhaps before all hear of his defilement, a quick dagger in the back may be best."

Regulus made no sound, no acknowledgement of these awful words, but he groaned deep inside.

Turning to Regulus, his tears having been prevented from falling by the lashes of his eyes, but with his eyes reddened and his voice gravelly and cracking, he said, "Thank you for your report, Regulus. You are a good friend. But I don't have the conviction of heart to see that Aurelius is worth saving. I feel more than disappointment in him. I feel contempt for him."

Regulus walked over to Claudius and placed his hands on his shoulders. With bowed heads, they both, guiding each other, sat down heavily.

"Marius speaks of this Jesus as if he is a real person—walking and talking with him, he says—not seeing him, but feeling his presence, he says. I don't know what that all means, but I…"

"Why worry with it, Regulus? They have rejected the old ways. Marius and Aurelius will come to their senses, recant these foolish thoughts of Jesus and his supposed resurrection, and all these other outrageous superstitions, or they are not Romans. If they are not Romans, they are not friends of Rome. They are, in fact, enemies of Rome," he said, now leaning close to Regulus.

"Without the State of Rome, we are nothing. Aurelius is nothing! Marius is nothing! Did we not learn this from our youth and did we not embrace this for ourselves and our families and swear it to Emperor Trajan in our last stint of service with Him? Trajan has accorded him such a high place. I shudder at what he will think!"

Regulus had heard enough. He dropped his efforts at diplomacy.

"We have been friends forever and we will always remain so. I feel as badly about our sons as you do. But if the feelings you are now exhibiting represent the spirit our gods give us in exchange for their favor, perhaps the cost is too expensive. When I think of Marius and I read the words of his letters about the love of Jesus, while I cannot accept his convictions, I can feel his sincerity and his genuine questions. It melts my heart and I yearn to sit with him, look him in the eyes, and reason with him…to try and correct him…not to…not to see him stabbed in the back. I hope I will get the chance to discuss these things with him at length when he returns from Rome."

"You will not, Regulus. The omens are against them, against Marius and Aurelius. They will not return to us. They have changed and will never be the same again. Entertain warm thoughts, if you will, Regulus, but I feel in my bones that what I have said will be the outcome of it all. The only real difference between our thinking this day is that you cling to the hope that the poison each of them drank will not kill them, and if drunk by more men, will not kill Rome. Call me bitter or stubborn, but in the end, you will wish that you had hardened earlier against Marius over this Christianity and have been done with it. Aurelius has written me three times, since his first letter, since I gave him my first, unconditional requirement, each time telling me that he will not write again unless I respond to him. But he has not recanted his wild beliefs, and, until and unless he does, what response can I make to him, in good conscience? I have therefore trashed his mail, and along with it I am trashing the memory of him." Looking sternly at Regulus, Claudius repeated his earlier declaration: "Aurelius is dead to me. My advice is to let Marius be dead to you. We must be who we are, Regulus. Be Romans!"

"Remember all the battles we fought and won for Rome, to make and keep the Roman way?" Regulus said sadly, "A man does not give up on his son so lightly after that; he fights to bring him back to Rome. When my heart has disagreed with the emperor and with my state, I have still fought for them. Why not fight for our sons, despite our deep differences with them? I will fight for Marius, and now, if you hold fast to your stubborn position, it appears that I will have to do the same for Aurelius without your blessings or help."

Regulus got up to leave.

"To stay the evening would mean to suffer more disappointment at your words. It has been a mostly pleasant visit, Claudius, and I want to carry that dominant memory with me. I will not grieve you further, nor let you grieve me."

Claudius seemed shocked at Regulus's blunt announcement.

"It may be good," Regulus added, "that the sins of the father may no longer be passed on to the son, as Marius tells me his new religion holds. Thus, our sons may escape our sins, and, if need be, their sons theirs."

"Regulus, I'm sorry you feel you have to leave. But you do not understand. These Christians are fanatics. They are lost to us, won by this Jesus and these Jesus people. They have given their new god all power over them. In Rome, we choose gods, depending on our felt need for them, and make sacrifices to them to bend their favor toward us. With this Jesus, Aurelius's letters say, Jesus chooses them and they accept him, without the offer of a sacrifice in exchange, because, he says, strangely, Jesus has made and at the same time is the sacrifice for them."

Now Regulus looked at Claudius inquisitively.

"Why the queer look, Regulus? Just because I do not respond to Aurelius's letters do not mean that I do not read them. They are… entertaining…and…child-like…like a curious fable. Who would, as Aurelius says Christianity teaches, gives his life to a god? As we know and have been taught, beyond sacrifices in wine and gold to our gods for favor to come or for past favors done, we owe them nothing more and nothing more is expected of us."

"I don't know, Claudius. Maybe it is as you say. Even so, my heart aches for my son. For an old man, like me, to be unsure of his gods is to admit a lifetime of mistakes and delusion. Marius doesn't see it that way. He says it doesn't matter what past beliefs have been or the past wrongs done, they are all forgiven, by accepting Jesus now. But, I…"

"Regulus! You think too much. You entertain too many questions, which if you don't stop will imperil all of our foundations. I had hoped not to pass on my sins and faults to my son, but that my honor and my traditions as a proud, unflinching Roman, admired in life and death by his colleagues and his countrymen, would be my legacy. That is being snatched from me by my own son! He has left me a man without a legacy, a poor man, indeed."

"The poorest in your thinking, Claudius, and perhaps in my own, also. For though I remain hopeful that Marius will return to me, sharing our religious observances and the Roman way, as before he left my immediate household to join the army, it is not because he has given me quarter to hope. Yet our religious legacies are not what either of them desires of us. In this they are making their own way, while still maintaining their undying allegiance to Rome. He tells me that this is their decision to live or die by and that he prays my acceptance. How can they prefer death, if it comes out of this new faith, more than living life with their sons—or, in the case of Aurelius, his sons to come? Claudius, we are both brave, and I have seen none braver than you. Yet their lack of fear is different from our bravery. Perhaps, we truly have nothing to pass on to them— blessings or curses. Perhaps, it is best that way—best that each man, whether father or son, bears the consequences of his own good works or his own iniquity."

"Sit down, my friend," Claudius said calmly. "Let us talk no more of these new threats, but just relive our old wars, perhaps livening our war stories with my best wines."

The old friends embraced again, extending their goblets to the slave girl for refills.

My three letters to my father went unanswered. I questioned the courier closely each time he returned empty handed, and each time the courier's look grew more sheepish, as he tried to save me from the rough messages my father had asked him to repeat to me. The embarrassed look of the courier, and the absence of return mail from my father, painted an unmistakable picture of rejection. My father stood on the one and only scathingly critical response he'd made to me two months ago. I still shed tears over my father's treatment of me, and I grapple with the unfamiliar challenge of not having my father, my rock and the source of approval of all I've done in my life, help me to navigate through the spiritual changes taking place within me...and, worse, now obviously disowning me. Then, Marius, sharing his father's report of his meeting with Claudius, jettisoned all remaining hope for our reconciliation. Marius's father's letter read:

> Marius. I hope you are well and in good spirits. I also hope that the gods have been with you and that you are protected. I worry about your neglect of them, for try as I have, I cannot grasp the notion of Jesus and Christianity. I continue to pass it off as your enchantment by this Ignatius, and believe that once you are out of his presence, and his spells, all will be well with us again on the matter of religion. Meanwhile, I am making sacrifices daily to the gods that you might be granted the wisdom of returning to your senses.

But you are my beloved son. I will always love you and wish the best for you. Even in this Jesus madness, you have tried to respectfully explain to me, in your own gentle way. May the gods forbid that you are wrong and I am right, because I would rather that I lose favor with them than you.

But my friend Claudius foams at the mouth like a rabid dog. He allows Aurelius no corner for questions about religion, dismissing his desire to talk matters over with him as if Aurelius were still a small boy.

Marius paused. "That is all I will read. That is enough, as I told you starting out that I would rather not share my father's letter with you.

"No. There is more. No matter how tough it is. I must know. Please, read on."

Marius took a deep breath and continued, "But more than that, I believe that Claudius has come to despise his son—even to curse him—even to entertain the ghastly idea that it may be better were Aurelius to die at the hands of Roman patriots to `abort the shame Aurelius will bring on his house, should all become known...'"

Marius stopped reading.

"I will read no more, Aurelius," Marius declared, resolutely.

<hr />

Later, as I told Ignatius of Marius's letter and my father's attitude toward me, he comforted me:

"Aurelius, these are the days of a new covenant that God promised in days of old, before Rome and the emperors, even before the pagan gods to which your father clings. No longer shall a man teach his son, saying, 'know the Lord' or 'this is our god,' for every man, through God's grace, and the shed blood of Jesus, shall know God, our true Father, for himself—from the least to the greatest. God said, 'I will put my word in their minds and write it on their hearts; and I will be their God and they will be my people.' You and I must pray for your father, that he repents and be forgiven; but you must hold fast to your own faith and the promises of God, Yahweh. While it is natural to want to please your father, only your personal belief in and relationship with Jesus matters."

Somewhat reassured, I still remained plainly sad.

"Listen to me," Ignatius said firmly but lovingly, "the stain of the sour grapes eaten by your father, Claudius, is washed away by the sweet sacrifice of Jesus for all. Let this taste of Jesus Christ be in your mouth, and it will be as manna from heaven—like the taste of a wafer made with honey."

CHAPTER 9
LITTLE GNAWING THINGS

"Take us the foxes, the little foxes, that spoil the vines: for our vines have tender grapes."
—Song of Solomon 2:15 (KJV)

In the privacy of his own room, free of the chains, the taunts, and the prying eyes of his soldier guards, Ignatius could meditate in solitude on the things of Jesus Christ and His church.

I did not see or learn of more stirring dreams or trances, leaving him unconscious to this world and seeming to have a foot in the next. But, this morning, as we watched the glow of the sunrise and the glistening tears of the dew, he told me more of the memories of his childhood meeting with Jesus. He told of those precious memories that again flooded his mind. His father took him to Jerusalem to meet and to be blessed by Jesus, he said. Jesus had been expected to arrive for weeks, but had detoured through Samaria on the way. More than twenty other fathers and boys waited with them.

Thinking on these things, Ignatius spoke aloud to me.

"Though only nearly four, I remember seeing Jesus sitting and teaching from atop a small knoll, a crowd gathered around Him. At an opportune moment when Jesus stopped speaking to greet some newcomers, my father and the rest of the men pushed us boys forward to meet Him and to ask for a blessing on our lives. At least three other boys and their fathers had traveled with my father and me from Antioch, Syria, a good distance, and our fathers were understandably anxious that our trip would not be in vain. We could not contain our spirited glee as we rushed to Jesus's knees. Though our fathers shushed us to be silent, I'm afraid we could not contain our excitement quietly. If they had really wished to have us remain stoic, then they should not have told us of the joy He would bring us upon our meeting Him. Our small disruption caught the annoyed attention of some of Jesus's disciples, who issued stern warning glares at us.

"I have tried to remember the face of Jesus as I saw it then, but I cannot recall anything except pure light. I know in reality it had to be like the bearded, sun-drenched dark face of any other man of Palestine, with brown eyes, curly hair, and a prominent nose, but try as I might, I cannot specifically recall it that way. I cannot even judge how tall He was, for He sat on a hill while we were in His presence, but I know He was not a giant physically, towering over men that day. I don't remember even His smile, because as we approached Him I recall an initial voice of agitation, which I at first thought to be directed at us children. Momentarily, though, it became plain that he aimed his displeasure at His disciples, who wanted to prevent our approaching Him, when we heard the tender words, "Suffer the little children to come unto me, and forbid them not…

But I do remember the warmth of His touch and the gentleness of His voice as He asked my name and the name of each child, tousled our hair, and invited us to serve Him and His Father in heaven. Lord, I can still hear Your voice today. I can still feel Your anointing touch and the power of your blessing on my life. I will soon be with You in Paradise."

"Ignatius! Ignatius!" I shouted, startling him. "You are not drifting into another one of your dreams, are you?"

"Oh, Captain Aurelius. Why must you interrupt me with silly questions? But no. I am not slipping into unconsciousness, just remembering with fondness. If you are blessed to grow as old as am I, you will learn the value of precious memories. May I ask you why you are shouting? Quiet is best. Listen, for God's voice. Anyway, shouting makes my old heart race. You do want me to live to make Rome, don't you?" Ignatius joked.

I quieted, for the thought of Rome saddened me. Ignatius saw that and tried to fix it.

"Aurelius. Aurelius. Remember. To die in the Lord is gain. Don't despair. Rejoice with me."

"I am. I am, Bishop. But it is not without pain, at least not yet. Besides, it was not my intention to scare you to death. To do so would destroy my mission. I'm usually very merciful to the aged," I said, trying to return Ignatius's laughter.

"And, I will make the same allowance for you, Ignatius, when you grow old," I snickered. "I once thought you old and frail, because of your look of skin and bones. But having witnessed your standing up under our brutality to you, and for a man of over eighty years, I know your God must be with you."

"My strength is in the Lord. I take no pride in self, because that is when the devil gains a foothold, when pride climbs up on the throne of our hearts. It is not the big things that we claim as our own doing that usually undermine us, for we may be on guard against them; it is the small things that trip us, more so, for they can go unnoticed, at least at first."

I stood transfixed, speechless, the wisdom and grace of Ignatius again amazing me.

"Are the other men coming? My spirit is light and joyous, this morning more than most, for I have filled my mind and heart to overflowing with thoughts of Jesus, and I feel a special move to share with all of you."

"Yes. Look, Marius, Dentatus, Valerius, Otho are approaching. Did you doubt your drawing power…old…well…old priest?"

Ignatius ignored my teasing.

"Welcome," he said to those arriving. "I hope, unlike your captain, Aurelius, you have come to study and not to engage in folly with me." They gave knowing looks, smiling at each other. "Well," Ignatius said, relenting, "I suspect even the good Lord enjoys a good laugh sometimes. How else could He put up with His people?"

Happy feelings abounded among Ignatius me, and these four men, today and every day that they met and discussed the things of God. But, Ignatius continually warned us that trials, a lot of pesky small ones, would come and test our newly confessed interest in committing to Jesus. He wanted to encourage us in the faith, but not to have us blithely believe that afflictions might not accompany our decision for Jesus—afflictions before which the best of us and our best intention might fail, unless we were solidly and prayerfully ready.

"God moves in mighty rushing winds that all can recognize and that none, even the most evil, can miss. But He also moves in still, small whispers, that only His children, His chosen and accepted, may hear. But the devil desires to make distractive noises, so that you do not hear God's small voiced urgings, avoiding attacking you where you are strong, but in weak places. This is done in the military warfare for which you are trained. You go for the exposed flank of the enemy, and then, as the enemy reacts to that hit, you may, with your enemy looking to his hurting weak flank, now attack and defeat what was previously thought to be his strong and impenetrable middle. It is what I think you in the military call a diversionary tactic. You will find, in your walk with Jesus, that the devil will more often than not attack you, not in big ways, but in smaller ones, that you might let in little things that allow him to accomplish his purpose—things like a little out-of-control tongue, quick anger, pride over a few things, or small lies, things you think you can handle on your own. But you must call on the help of the Holy Spirit even for these. A new faith, strengthened through constant prayer, can guard you against these little foxes creeping in."

"More riddles, Ignatius?" Valerius asked. "I try and understand what I must do to be as you are, but you will not talk plainly. As a soldier, I am used to having my requirements made plain."

"I feel the same," Otho joined in. "I am coming to desire to have faith as you have instructed—that Jesus is the Son of God and that He is resurrected, and that men who believe in Him are saved to eternal life—and that those who do not are eternally damned. Before, you have said that was enough. Are you now speaking in circles about little foxes and new requirements? Are we to be called foxes, to guard against ourselves?"

"No. No. No. I do not add a new requirement. But you are newly exploring Christian faith, and your faith must take root and grow, else it will be lost, and you will fall back, perhaps to where you began. You are well familiar with the habits of foxes, slyly moving in on their prey, I am sure. But little foxes present a different challenge. They are not yet big enough to chase down hares or kill a full-grown gander. So the little fox creeps in to unguarded places, virtually unde-tected because of his size, and destroys, requiring no speed or skill or courage to kill. For example, he attacks the defenseless roots of vineyards by gnawing on them. That is what can happen in your life, in the case of fear, or the worry of disappointing others, or just hav-ing old bad habits—little sinful practices creep back in. You must be vigilant, through prayer, to ask God to help you see and catch these little foxes at the gates of your vineyards, your minds and hearts, so that your faith may grow in strength."

"Ignatius, do you see something in our futures, mine or the oth-ers, here?" Valeris implored, "Little foxes creeping in to destroy us?"

"They are always coming, my children. Be aware. Watch and pray, for they are surely coming."

Ignatius kept his light mood no matter our questions. Looking over our faces and fielding our child-like inquires, seemed to excite him, giving him the chance to teach us more and more about serving Jesus, while making us more and more aware that we were like tender grapes that, were we not careful and prayerful, would not survive to harvest, dying on the vine, spoiled by little foxes gnawing at our young roots. Maybe it would be a fear, or a lie, or an old habit, or maybe not enough prayer and Scripture. He couldn't tell who or which it would be, he said.

"I love each of you dearly, though sometimes, when I reflect on the little time I have to teach you about the things of Jesus, a tear drops in my heart," he said sadly. Perhaps our faith would fail along this trip. If not along the way to Rome, though, then surely the five of us, newly converted or on our ways toward conversion to believ-ing in and depending on Jesus, would have to meet Trajan in Rome. There we might have to choose whether either would consume us, the little foxes or the lions.

CHAPTER 10
THE PLOTTERS AND THE PLOT

*"The wicked plotteth against the just, and gnasheth
upon him with his teeth."*
—*Psalm 37:12 (KJV)*

Publius did not descend from a man of rank in the Roman military, but came from one of the lower classes of Roman society. His start in the army did not come through the recommendation of a senator, consul, or any man of position. He received no training in military fitness and tactics at an early age, preparing him for a career of excellence. A crude and cruel man, his father used his rough, club-like hands to shoe horses, tear down building walls, and beat him. And if those hands did not administer his beatings, then the hard leather reins, taken from the horse stables, did the job. His father's voice, accompanying his beatings, echoed throughout Publius's life. Publuis's severe beatings led him to see violence as an answer to address every problem he faced in life, and caused him a mental condition that required him to fight against voices in his head that repeatedly steered him toward violent acts.

"You're too headstrong, boy. I am gonna beat you 'til I break you. I am gonna make you a man!" These condemning words, shouted by Publius' father, Felix, accompanied virtually every blow that Publius was forced to absorb at father's hands.

A clumsy child, Publius had to work hard at learning agility. Other children, even those in his own lower class, chided him over his unkempt looks and awkwardness. They looked down on him, for his own shortcomings and also for those of his father, an uncouth drunkard with a foul mouth. So, Publius fought them. He fought them all. He stayed alert to slights and he punished everyone whom he felt guilty of one toward him or his father. He hated just about everyone and was angry at everyone, except his father, whom he forgave for everything he did to him, for he loved him and craved his love in return. His greatest desire was to make his father proud of him and to prove all those who teased or denied him and his father their friendship wrong, very wrong, about their predictions that he would not amount to much. So Publius set his sights on joining the Roman army, a road that many simple men before him had traveled to glory.

In the earlier days of the Roman Empire, a boy with Publius's background would never have been admitted to the army of Rome. But scores of wars had depleted the ranks of the young men of families of property and position, so that both their numbers and their lack of taste for the sacrifices of war—the length of service and the hardships—opened up opportunity and demand for volunteers. Even the chance for volunteers did not provide a clear path for Publius, for he was short of stature by Roman army standards. While a man like Aurelius would have not had his opportunity to serve limited by his height, because he would have been accepted as the son of a centurion, no such exception was available to Publius. Moreover, at well over six feet tall, Aurelius would not have needed it. Publius, no more than five feet, seven inches tall—the acceptable height for a volunteer being five feet, ten inches—was saved from failing this requirement by the happenstance of having his examination for admission to the service fall at the same time and place as that of a reluctant Christian who was being levied into the army against his will.

"What is your name?" the consul asked the Christian.

"What does it matter? I am a Christian and my faith does not permit me to bear arms."

"Well, we will see about that. You will be outfitted and take your oath today!" the consul insisted. "Tell me your name or you will be flogged until you do!"

"It is Apion, sir. But, I cannot serve in the army. I cannot do evil. I am a Christian."

"Measure him!" the consul ordered.

His staff assistant complied, but reported after measuring Apion: "Sir. He is only five feet, eight inches. Below the required standard."

"Give him the military seal and place it on a chain around his neck anyway. His cowardly protests annoy me."

"He will accept the seal and the chain now or you will torture him until he does. Failing that, I will turn him over to my executioner."

As Apion kept up his protest, insisting that whether dressed forcibly, flogged, or executed, he would not serve as a soldier, Publius, knowing he was even shorter than Apion, saw and seized his chance.

"Then take me in his place, Honorable Consul. I will fight to the death for Rome. Why waste your uniform and your sacred seal on this reluctant one? I have learned in my nineteen years, as I have defeated many men much taller than I in battles with both my fists and weapons, that too much attention is paid to height. It may be, Honorable Consul, that a brave soldier may prove more valuable than a tall one."

The recruitment chamber exploded in raucous laughter at this muscle-bound little guy taking charge, the consul leading the laughter. When decorum was finally restored, the consul declared Publius fit for service.

"Take the military seal from around the neck of this coward, who calls himself a Christian. Have him heavily flogged. And let him thank this…what is your name, son?

"Publius, sir. Publius Capito."

"Yes. Thank Publius for creating an atmosphere of levity for you, Christian, Apion, or whatever you are, for my thought, immediately before Publius spoke, was to order your execution, forthwith. I will now reduce that to heavy, heavy flogging, because I cannot impose a penalty of death while in the midst of laughter."

"Give his seal to Publius, who I am sure will wear it proudly and courageously. Measure him for a uniform. Who is your father, Publius?"

"You would not know him, Honorable Consul. He is a simple blacksmith's assistant, and a man who, before that, served as a carpenter to some, making repairs to living quarters."

"That being the case," the consul said, clearing his throat, "you are assigned to the Cavalry of the Sixth cohort of the Tenth Legion. There are walls to be built and horses to be shod. Do well there and you will soon mount a steed in defense of Rome and in conquest of her enemies. May the gods protect you."

Publius's father, who had never had any confidence in him, now exuded great pride at his selection to the army, boasting of his son and his household as defenders of Rome. He gave him a modest dinner with his neighbors as a sendoff and spoke kindly to him for the first time in his life.

After several months in the Army, Publius wrote to his father:

> Dear Father,
>
> Things are going well for me. I have received two high compliments from my commander for my tireless work and progress in my training. I will send you and my sister a part of my earnings to help with your upkeep.
>
> Conditions here are difficult, but I have no complaints. I used to hate the hard way you raised me, but the truth is it prepared me for this hardship—for any hardship: the mud, the snow, the discipline, the pain—and while I thrive against these elements, some other soldiers faint. Thank you for that training and for bringing me up around horses and dogs. I have not only impressed my commanders because my eyes are alert, my head is erect, my chest broad, my shoulders muscular, my waist slim, and my legs sinewy and strong, and by outworking any two men, but I am able to talk to these horses and dogs in ways to get them to perform that confounds my commanders and my fellow soldiers. They have no

clue as to how I do it, or that it comes from the many nights you required me to sleep in the stables with these animals when I could not follow your orders as I should have.

I believe I will advance quickly. I am told that in several months to come I may be able to make a portrait in my uniform that I can send home. Please tell your friends about my success and those men who I grew up with and who doubted me. I will write you later and please write me and tell me of your welfare. May the gods be with you.

Your son,
Publius

Publius's letter arrived just before the death of his father, who was killed in an accident involving the furnace he used to soften and bend iron horseshoes. Publius would not go to the funeral and could not accept his death. Given all he was doing to bring pride to his father and pride to his father's household, his death added to Publius's anger against the world. He could no longer share his success with his father face-to-face, so he would do it vicariously for him. He comforted himself in the knowledge that his father died with the treasure of the one letter he had received from him. Forthwith, he would keep him in his heart, buried deep within, along with the bitter memory of the way in which he and his father were cheated in life. He would use that, along with every other blow he had been dealt, to fuel his ambition.

Publius's mastery with horses, getting them to charge steadfastly in the face of any danger and to maneuver brilliantly on command, soon catapulted him out of the dank blacksmith shops and wood-making sheds, to lead the training of cavalry horses and riders full-time. This created, not too much later, his chance to ride and fight on horseback. From this vantage point, he made a name for himself and earned the nickname, "The Bull on Horseback." He led one of the most successful cohorts of the Tenth Legion, in terms of battles won, that the legion had ever seen. He and his men charged over enemy positions, taking them out without regard to his personal safety or that of his men. Though this mode of fighting had serious drawbacks, with his troops and his steeds taking more casualties than those of any other cohort, his victories made him part of a core of up-and-coming young military leaders to be reckoned with. In the Legio X, that core also included Aurelius and Marius.

Publius hated Aurelius almost from the moment he met him and came to know him as the son of a centurion. His stout, pale ruggedness contrasted poorly with Aurelius's tall, ruddy handsomeness. Aurelius's easy style made him more likeable than Publius's gruffness. Publius had made himself a success by dint of his own hard work and by overcoming early handicaps, while, as he saw it, Aurelius had made his way up the ladder through connections in high places. And though Publius tried to take pride in the accomplishments of which he could take ownership, still his pride sagged in the charismatic presence of Aurelius. Lacking true confidence, he always feared that he could lose position and slide back into a life of oblivion. From Publius's perspective, he supposed that Aurelius had no such fears, for he saw him as protected by the reputation of his father, Claudius, and the ties that went all the way to Emperor Trajan himself. Though Aurelius was personally a highly skilled and aggressive soldier, putting himself in harm's way without fear, Publius discounted Aurelius's qualities as a reason for his advancements. Aurelius's highly honed abilities Publius attributed to the expensive advantage in training his father bought for him as a boy.

"While I have struggled to make myself a first-rate soldier, Aurelius has waltzed into position through the influence and tutoring of his father. He is ahead of me in advancements, not because he is more capable or more courageous but simply because he was born luckier," Publius seethed.

The advantage of connections to high authorities and the contribution that played in Aurelius's meteoric rise were undeniable. But a few other young soldiers, standing toe-to-toe with Aurelius in performance, were not held back in the face of directly competing against him. Those who were his equal in the field were transferred out of the Legio X and were now in charge of their own centuries, centurions in their own right. But in the case of Publius, commanders made no such decisions. They knew too well of his dark disposition, that his men feared but did not revere him, and that his peers could not trust him. He had a reputation for impishness, flashing into anger at the slightest provocation, making his commanders wary of his capacity to make mature, clear-headed decisions under duress, a flaw that could put thousands of men and their missions in unnecessary jeopardy, were he in charge of making calls for large numbers of men. These intrinsic flaws, which he neither recognized in himself nor appreciated when they were pointed out by others, were the principal reasons why his advancement had come to a standstill. Bravery in a soldier, it had turned out, unfortunately, was enough for an ordinary soldier or for one with a small command, but not enough to warrant the high advancement in the army that he desired and to which he felt entitled. His insufferable upbringing had made him hard, fearless, driven, and able to withstand harsh punishment, but it had forever robbed him of self-confidence, generosity, warmth, and good judgment. He twisted reality to make his father's cruelty to him a virtue, for his greatest fear was admitting to himself that his father did not care for him. Rudderless after his father died, he drove himself hard by blind ambition to please a father who had shown signs of affection for him only because he'd joined the army.

He would give the posthumous gift of a successful army career to his father by any means necessary, taking on anyone in his way.

Aurelius shocked him by asking him to join the mission of escorting Ignatius to Rome. Flattered, he called a truce in his heart with him, feeling that, in spite of his longstanding hatred for Aurelius, Aurelius recognized his abilities. Besides, he reckoned, the mission, being of high importance to Emperor Trajan, might give him the chance to make some relationship with him, independent of Aurelius. But now, after what he considered Aurelius's over-the-top attacks on him in front of his colleagues a few nights ago, he was back to square one with him, loathing the ground on which

Aurelius walked and wishing him dead. Yet, something was different in this season of hostility toward Aurelius. This season presented him the chance to make a deeper connection with Trajan than he ever could have thought possible. Furthermore, he didn't have to think about stabbing Aurelius in the dark, or poisoning him with the poison he carried with him that he used to take out the horses of enemy soldiers, or hire someone else to do the dirty deed. No, in one fell swoop, the chance presented itself for him to short-circuit Aurelius's career, if not his life, and to advance his own, in the form of a grateful reward from Trajan.

Although Publius was unaccustomed to thinking through clandestine palace plots, his skill set lying more in brute strength, this one appeared obvious. He knew that Aurelius had spoken truthfully when he'd said that Trajan would not believe him, were he to send him a letter stating that Aurelius should be removed from command because he'd professed to have been persuaded by his prisoner to become a Christian. "After all," he reasoned to himself, "who am I, a soldier unknown to Trajan, to expect to bring Aurelius down through a mere accusation, when Trajan trusted Aurelius, and his father before him, with his very life.

"After being met with disbelief, my letter might also stir Trajan's anger against me, as a soldier disloyal to his captain and unworthy of higher rank."

"No, I will bide my time until I get to Rome. In the meantime, I will cultivate my relationship with Antonius, Minucius, Quintas, and Ruffinus and show them the benefits of making our disclosures to Trajan about these Christian traitors in the right way, at the right place and at the right time. At a time and in a way when our veracity and loyalty to the army and to Trajan cannot be called into question."

After standing beneath the stars and making these uncharacteristically sound judgments, Publius started out for his room, still immersed in his tentative notions of a new career plan for himself, his friends, and his enemies. Aurelius was the main target, the head of the snake that had to die, but Marius would be unavoidable collateral damage. As he entered the barracks, his mind occupied with his plotting, he literally bumped into Aurelius and Marius, who were standing in the doorway to the barracks, talking.

"Oh, excuse me, Aurelius, Marius. I didn't see you there."

"We saw you coming, Publius, and wondered if the Bull would run us over, since you kept coming directly toward us, seemingly oblivious to our standing here," Marius said, smiling.

"Yes," I said. "We thought you might be going to do us in. But I couldn't believe that even you would dare try and take both of us out at the same time, at least not unless we were both asleep," I continued to joke.

"No. No need to worry about that, Captain Aurelius, nor you, Marius. I am not one to hold a grudge. So, please excuse me and goodnight."

And Publius walked away calmly.

"I'm not sure I like the new, polite Publius," Marius finally said, as Publius disappeared around a corner. "I think he bears watching."

"Then watch him, Marius. I'm at peace." I said dismissively.

———•———

Publius sat at the table in his quarters, took out his papyrus, and starting writing a letter to his father. He did this whenever he made a good success or felt he was about to do so. He still wanted to make him proud, even though his father had been dead for twenty years.

"Dear Father," Publius wrote,

> The gods have delivered my enemies into my hands. I feel your shadow near me, applauding me from the underworld, and I know that you are reading over my shoulder. These clever boys, Aurelius and Marius, have outsmarted themselves, turning to atheism and denying the gods whom we worship, whom Emperor Trajan worships, even turning from Emperor Trajan himself. Remember that Christian's life I saved that I told you about on the day I was selected to join the army? Well,

he was the first and is the last Christian I will ever spare. In this, I will gain the esteem of Emperor Trajan and all Rome, for me and for your household, esteem that will last forever.

Your son,
Publius

That done, Publius opened his large duffel bag and unpacked a few clothing items. Then he dropped his letter to his father into it, pressing it down tightly on top of dozens of other letters he had written to his father over the years.

CHAPTER 11

STIRRING DISCORD

"These…things doth the Lord hate… An heart
that deviseth wicked imaginations…"
—Proverbs 6:16, 18 (KJV)

We covered more than nine hundred miles from Antioch to Troas,
and, with various planned stops and meetings between Ignatius
and others, it had taken us from mid-April to mid-October to do
it. The cities of Neapolis, just on the border of the Roman province of Macedonia, and Philippi, about a hundred miles farther east,
two emerging strongholds of the Christian faith, lay ahead as our
next destinations. My goal was to reach Rome early in the next year,
before the scheduled military celebratory festivities in March. To
ensure keeping that schedule, I planned to make stops in Neapolis
and Philippi, and then move on to Thessalonica, the latter a good
place to winter my men. Sailing to Rome in the late fall and winter months was inadvisable, because of predictably strong and severe
tempests. With a goodly number of Christians in each of these cities,
they were originally picked as points at which to pause in order to
carry out one of my principal original goals—to parade and embarrass Ignatius before his Christian base and to have the word of that
thereafter spread among Christians so that they would realize their
weakness and forever fear incurring the wrath of Rome, in general,
and of Trajan, in particular.

Though, perhaps more than half of my men eagerly desired to
pursue this objective, I and others of them now found it futile. For

my part, I also found it undesirable. In any event, no matter how brutally and condescendingly we treated Ignatius, whether along the way, in open areas or in churches, he appeared immune to feelings of humiliation. Indeed, the more we disparaged him before his church members, the more strength he and they seemed to gain, he and they declaring their attitude toward suffering to confirm, rather than ridicule, the value of their lives and works as Christians. Our path to Rome, in the light of our actions, stabilizing rather than unnerving Ignatius's followers, should have been a straight line that avoided Christian communities. But, we couldn't change routes now, or to sufficiently explain the reasons why to Crassus and Emperor Trajan.

Crossing into Macedonia, we rolled onto the wide and brilliantly constructed Via Egnata, the Roman road that connected the continent of Asia to Europe. Built around 130 BC, it ran a distance of around five hundred miles from the point at which we entered it to the city of Dyrrachium, located on the coast of the Mediterranean Sea. I would have to later decide whether to go through Dyrrhachium to Rome or take a ship in Thessalonica, but that decision lay a few months ahead. Though intended as a military roadway, the Via Egnata had long since also become the international route for commerce and travel in the region. Busy and crowded with merchants and travelers, still, our troop of splendidly dressed soldiers, armed to the hilt, riding on handsome mounts, and exuding a thick air of authority, stood out. Travelers gawked at our impressive display of pomp and power, and probably at the peculiarity of our contingent dragging a single, chained, skinny, old priest.

The churches in Neapolis and Philippi received Ignatius warmly and enthusiastically. The news of his coming obviously preceded him, perhaps from members of the churches in the cities we'd passed through running ahead of us to spread the news that we might pass through their areas. These Christian groups welcomed Ignatius with cries of "God-bearer! Bless you God-bearer," as he entered churches in homes or other small places of assembly. Those present listened to him intently, either curious to soak up his wisdom or wanting to ask him questions that forced him to recount his experiences with Jesus's disciples. They doted on him, treating him like a newly discovered, treasured elder nearing death, who they were being given a final chance to experience. Ignatius spoke modestly, insisting on a lack of interest on his part in taking credit for the steadfastness he showed in dealing with the extraordinary stresses of his journey toward the horrible fate awaiting him in Rome. Giving all credit to God, for his strength and endurance seemed to endear him to his Christian colleagues even more.

Ignatius's prominently displayed his fearlessness when we reached Philippi. The Via Egnata ran right through it, too, making it as commercially significant as Neapolis. Named for the father of Alexander the Great, Philippi served as a gateway to east and west Macedonia. In fact, the gate on the eastern side of Philippi had written upon it, "Neapolis Gate," and the gate on its west side was called the Kneenides Gate, referring to a city west of it in the direction of the sea. Philippi uniquely tested Ignatius and his fellow Christians because it was heavily populated by former soldiers of the Roman military.

Founded in 42 BC after a decisive battle was fought on its site, Philippi was dedicated by Emperor Octavia in 27 BC, a Roman military retirement colony, "the Colony Julia Augusta Philippensis." The retirees who lived here felt an intense loyalty to Rome and an unparalleled devotion to its deities, whom they credited with seeing them through the dangers of war. Their enmity toward Christians, whom they perceived as standing against everything they stood for, remained palpable.

Christians in Philippi had never celebrated their faith so openly as when Ignatius came to town. Their enthusiastic meetings and sounds of praise reverberated throughout the city, arousing the ire of many a military retiree. Differences between Ignatius's Christians way of life and the way of life of some veterans led to a few small but open clashes, and to loud calls by a sizeable segment of the military retirement community to muzzle the Christians' activities. This, in turn, led a few wavering Christians to urge Ignatius to take his speeches and their worship services underground. He wouldn't hear of it.

"If we do not hold Jesus Christ up before men, then who will be the instruments to draw men to belief in Him?" Ignatius asked.

"Did God not instruct Moses, even as poisonous snakes bit at the Israelites' heels, to have his people look up at His own bronze serpent and live? Now we are privileged to look upon Him on His cross and live. So, let the vipers bite. We shall live! We shall live with our heads toward heaven!"

Publius could hardly stomach Ignatius's defiance. Each day in Philippi, he strained to control his anger. He often heard voices that egged him toward violent actions, and those voices kept screaming one directive, "Kill Ignatius!" He struggled to control them. "What would it matter to Trajan, once you explain yourself to your emperor?" argued these voices in justification. Whenever these feelings, these thoughts, arose within him, Publius fought them hard, squeezing his head in his hands and crushing the voices until they quieted.

"Murder of one's commander is a hideous and unforgiveable thing under Roman law. To kill Ignatius, you would have to kill Aurelius as well, for he would fight you to the death. We would both pay dearly, with our own lives, were we guilty of that, no matter our reasons. I share your abhorrence of Ignatius, and especially of his new protector and apologist, Aurelius, for Aurelius abandons the purpose of our mission and spits in the face of every god of Rome," Antonius counseled Publius. "Though I can throw the javelin accurately at fifty yards, I have learned that it is sometimes wiser to let your enemy come in close and surprise him with repeated jabs, not just from your lance but from the lances and swords of the men on your side. We need more of his troop to turn against him, and that will require patience."

"I am unaccustomed to playing this patience game. I know you speak well, but it is hard to wait it out," Publius replied.

"But we must let it play out. I pray you. We must seek to encourage the retirees at every opportunity, encourage them to pressure Ignatius and the Christians, through Aurelius, to tone down the Christians' exhortations—and to ask why his prisoner goes about practically unchained, except for light, loose chains on his ankles. I suspect Aurelius will try to defend Ignatius and his fellow Christians. We will both bear witness against him, and let the soldiers know that Aurelius fancies himself a Christian. And, too, by our actions we may encourage Ruffinus, Decimus, and the others to fall more solidly in with us, wholly against Aurelius and Marius. They lean toward us presently. These further actions will push them firmly into our camp."

Publius and Antonius had the makings of a good pair. They matched each other in hatred for Aurelius, Marius, and Ignatius, but were opposites in temperament. That difference in temperament was a good and necessary thing, because all fire, if it is to be employed in useful purpose, must be brought under some governance. Antonius possessed negotiating skills that Publius lacked and that Publius did not usually appreciate. He assigned himself the task, with the blessing of Publius, of keeping Ruffinus, Minucius, Quintas, and Decimus aligned with them, two of whom had tentatively indicated a desire to do so when they walked out of the meeting with them following the violent argument between Publius and Aurelius a month or so earlier. Then, Antonius had a special connection with Dentatus from their competitions in spear and javelin tossing. Both champions, they had fought earlier and worked side by side in a company of spearmen. That company of spearman had been commanded by Aurelius, which was why, in significant part, Antonius reasoned, Dentatus had not left the meeting with him and Publius when the others had, for he knew Dentatus to be extremely pious regarding the gods of Rome, and an extremely loyal soldier. He now simply had to show him that his ultimate loyalty rested with Rome, not with his immediate captain, who by his disloyalty to Rome had abandoned any rightful claim to his place of leadership in the Roman army—ergo, to dishonor him was not to dishonor Rome; quite the opposite. Getting Dentatus on their side would potentially give he and Publius a split of Aurelius's men of six to four in their favor, if not against Aurelius generally, then certainly against him on the matter of Aurelius's views on Christianity.

Antonius approached Dentatus as he sat alone in his quarters.

"Are you thinking...or as Ignatius would say, meditating, on your new god?" he coyly began with Dentatus.

"I don't know the new god of which you speak. These are confusing times. Ignatius tells me that men worship many gods—whichever things they hold dearest in their hearts—but he says that there is only one true god, Yahweh. But I don't have to tell you this. You already know that. Why do you ask, Antonius? Are you seeking a confession from me so that I may be brought to suffer for my thoughts?"

"No, Dentatus. That would never be my motive. We are brothers—literally brothers of the same arms. I wasn't thinking about Ignatius's god, really, though I cannot deny the dangers of a soldier worshipping him. I was more thinking along the lines of Ignatius preaching to you that men can worship many gods and unwittingly make a god anything we worship that we ought not. My essential question to you, then, dear Dentatus, before I would ask of your consideration of Ignatius's god, is whether you have made Aurelius your god?"

Dentatus looked confused, so Antonius bore in.

"You needn't answer that now. Think about it. It is good to follow your captain, but captains change. The gods of Rome stay the same, and so will the Roman Empire. Except for the emperor, himself a deity, no man deserves unstinting loyalty—especially one whose actions may undermine the gods of the state, which is to say the state itself. I am not talking about mutiny. But the time may come when you may be called to a decision between Rome and Aurelius. It may not be a decision that ripens on this journey to Rome, but once in Rome...well...one never knows. Please, as your friend, I sincerely urge you to earnestly apply yourself to thinking these things through."

Dentatus returned a thoughtful look, considering Antonius's advice. Then, he answered quietly.

"Thank you, Antonius. You are a good friend."

Antonius and Dentatus clasped hands firmly, Antonius smiling widely.

Emperor Augustus initiated the practice of veteran's superannuation, special outlays paid to retiring veterans either in cash or in a plot of land. This superannuation could be paid to an individual retiree, or the payments could be made to an organized military colony. The makeup of the Roman army, manned mostly by soldiers from places other than Italy, resulted in many veterans settling in lands outside of Italy, in the countries of their origins or of their last postings. Philippi established a good number of veteran colonies. Cavalrymen, infantrymen, and archers made up the ranks of most of these veterans, all of whom held extremely conservative views on anything that portended change, especially in religious matters. Some of the most senior veterans had fought and bore battle scars from the Jewish-Roman wars, and these men still made no distinction between Jews and Christians, seeing that the Christian cult came from the Jews. Christians were, at best, the same troublemakers as their step-parents and, at worst, a new and greater threat to security—enemies of the state, the lot of them. Those veterans who had been granted the high privilege of Roman citizenship because of military service had recited long oaths of loyalty and allegiance to Rome and its divine emperors and other gods. Veterans of this stripe, and they made up most of the colonies of veterans in Philippi, felt viscerally obligated to Rome, more than most, and wore their patriotism on their chests.

Lucius and Iallius, twenty-five years in the service of the Thracian Archers, serving in the Third Cohort of Legio V, bristled at the spectacle of Christians rallying in support of Ignatius, whom they discovered was a condemned criminal and with the reputation of an unrepentant and fanatical atheist. Ignatius, these soldiers found out, was condemned by the direct order of Emperor Trajan. This convinced them that Ignatius was an enemy to the State. How could it be otherwise when one so honorable as Trajan had seen fit to personally send him to his death? They concluded that something had to be done, and immediately.

The soldiers also learned that my father and I were held in high esteem by Trajan. Therefore, it made sense to them to deal with Ignatius's incitement of the Christian community, through a meeting with me. I eagerly responded to their request to meet with me. I did not expect a hard meeting, in fact I expected they would approach me with great deference on account of both my father and Trajan.

"Captain Aurelius, we are indeed pleased to meet you. We have heard a great number of very impressive things about your military service and leadership, for which we are grateful. We have also heard that you are your father's son and that warms our hearts greatly." Lucius began, opening our discourse.

"It is my pleasure to greet you. For, whatever my service to Rome may be, it is your service that made mine possible, so I am the one in your debt," I replied, humbly. I could not bear to respond to the intended compliment regarding my father, as I feared that it might engender further discussion about he and I, and my pain over my father's rejection of me was still too raw.

"That is very gracious of you, Captain. But we are here with a serious concern, one which we hope you will help us address. We are deeply offended by this Bishop Ignatius, so-called, who is going about our city spreading false doctrine and disrupting life here. Also, we do not understand why a prisoner, as dangerous as he is proving himself to be, is not always heavily chained, as has been every other prisoner we have ever seen transported through our city. Both these things are obnoxious to the veterans' colonies here—more than five thousand veterans—and, frankly, we want both Ignatius and his message gagged and bound. Iallius, I, and these few men are representatives of our veterans' communities, and on behalf of them, we ask this relief. May I report back to our group that you will honor our requests?"

I considered the faces and words of these good men, faces that showed a genuineness of spirit that I identified with men the age of my own father. My admiration grew.

"It is very good to be in your company," I found myself reiterating. "I understand your concerns and I respect the manner in which you have expressed them. You have sacrificed so much for Rome. But to your points. This mission started out with Ignatius heavily shackled daily and every minute of the day—chains holding his ankles, his wrists, and around his waist. I did it because I worried that he might try and escape or that some Christian sympathizer might try and free him from our troop. Through experience over the past six or seven months, I have determined that neither of these is a present concern.

Ignatius is, indeed, surprisingly, zealous in his desire to be sacrificed to the lions in Rome, and his Christian friends are complete pacifists, unwilling to bear arms, even under the threat of execution. Furthermore, Ignatius is more than eighty years old. The chains are very heavy and the season is hot."

"That may be, Captain," Iallius replied, "but he is a prisoner and undeniably a dangerous one. He would not be on his way to be executed were the emperor not of the conviction that he is a threat to Rome, a dangerous man. Bind him to the fullest extent. Treat him as the apparent traitor that he is. Make him to suffer the heaviest chains possible. Is that not the way that the Roman Army treats prisoners sentenced to death?"

"I cannot say that you are incorrect, dear sir," I began. "It is the way that I have treated every prisoner in the past, and I have not cared whether the prisoner lived or died in my custody. However, in this case, I must present this prisoner alive in Rome, as the emperor desires to make a gross example of how he treats the leaders of outlawed clubs—like Christian clubs—who do not recognize or respect the gods of Rome. Therefore, I must exercise leniency, unusual leniency, given Ignatius's age, so that I am not harder on him than his constitution can bear. That is why I have not subjected him to the grossest treatments possible. I trust you accept my words and understand my position."

I looked them in the eyes without blinking.

Continuing, I said, "I do not now, and never will, let anything stand between me and my duty to deliver this prisoner alive to the teeth of the lions in Rome. My resolve in that regard is as hard as iron. Make no mistake about that. And, as an officer of the Roman Army, I pledge my honor to you on that. I would think that is a sufficient response."

My response was so steely and so convicting that it seemed I saw all the men wince, and say in their hearts, "What a soldier." Then, Lucius offered meekly, "And, to the other part of our request?"

"The meetings with Christians were authorized by Emperor Trajan, himself, through his executive attaché, Crassus. They are intended as a part of our mission, to observe his behavior and theirs, in the interest of planning for the security of the state," I said firmly.

"But does this latter point have to mean that he may speak out against the gods of Rome, even exhort his followers to dishonor them, in order for you to make the observations that you say you are charged to make?" Lucius continued.

"In speaking for his God, he necessarily speaks against the gods of Roman tradition, for he believes, and his faith teaches, that there is only one God."

I looked them in the eyes without blinking. Then, I continued.

"I do not now, and I never will, let anything stand between me and my duty to Emperor Trajan regarding this prisoner. My resolve in this regard is unshakeable. Make no mistake about that," I solemnly concluded.

"What may we tell those who sent us, then, Captain, you appearing to us believing that all is well?"

"Tell them that all is well and that I will find a way to respect their wishes." Then the light of a concluding idea gave me my ultimate way out.

"Gentlemen, here is my final assurance to you that you need not worry further about the problems Ignatius presents in your city. In about two days hence, my troop and I will depart Philippi on the way to Thessalonica. Tell them that I will resolve this matter in that way."

Smiles and nods of satisfaction spread across the room, all satisfied that I had worked things out in a final and respectful manner. They prepared to leave, satisfied with themselves, at what they had apparently accomplished in the meeting with me, and very happy that their contact with Ignatius would be soon over. As they were saying their good-byes, Publius burst into the room.

"Forgive me, honorable veterans, Captain Aurelius. Have you all had your questions cleared up?"

"Yes. Yes, we have. He's been quite generous with his time. But what business is it of yours? Are you not his subordinate?"

Beads of sweat rolled down my brow. I wiped them away, wondering if the veterans noticed a confusing change in my composure.

"I am Publius, a part of Captain Aurelius's troop, to be sure. Has he told you of his high opinion of Ignatius?"

"Publius! You are out of order. I command you to dismiss yourself from this gathering and to apologize to our guests," I shouted, recovering.

"Yes, sir. Yes, sir," Publius complied, saluting smartly with a silly smile on his face, under the dark glare of the veterans. "Sorry, gentlemen. I just wanted to be sure nothing was left out."

Publius then left, but waited at the door through which the veterans were obliged to exit.

"What was the cause of that intrusion, Captain?" Lucius asked. "What an impudent soldier. Why, in my day, he would have been severely flogged or had several vine staff's broken across his back. The army is growing soft. Discipline is breaking down. I worry about that. I think we all do. See to his disrespect, Captain. Good day, Captain," Lucius said, in resignation.

"Psst. Psst! Sirs!" Publius whispered, catching the old soldiers going out. "Aurelius did not give you straight answers. He is not just a Christian sympathizer, coddling Ignatius and tolerating his insults of our gods, he is one of them. Aurelius is a Christian."

To a man they stood shocked.

"Believe me. It is true. You should get word to Rome about it."

"Publius. That is your name?" Lucius demanded.

"Yes. Yes, sir."

"Of what household are you?"

Publius swallowed hard. "My father is dead and he was a simple man, while he lived. My household is of no note and, for these present purposes, of no matter," Publius answered with a tone of disrespect, hurt by the question.

"It is good that your father will not hear of your behavior, for were he a veteran like one of us, he would suffer disgrace, for you disgrace the uniform of our state. Such disrespect for a superior officer I have not seen in my nearly fifty-five years of association with the military. No emperor of Rome would put a Christian in charge of this exclusive mission, this unit. Perhaps they would order him to the front ranks to die, but that is the only place of leadership an

137

emperor would accord to a Christian. No. We do not want to hear more. Good day, unless you want to stand in the way of veterans and deny our departure," Lucius finished dressing down Publius, pressing against him to pass through the doorway.

They rushed away, the hard flopping of their sandals against the stones of the barrack yard making a steady, hasty beat.

Publius grew weak in the knees. Antonius had told him to simply watch out for the veteran's approach, notify him. await him, and they would, together, talk with them before they entered the meeting with Aurelius. Together, they would attempt to gain their support—the support of all in the colonies—to register a complaint to the offices of Emperor Trajan against Aurelius. This way, they would till the ground for the grave of Aurelius when they reached Rome. Antonius and Publius had even joked about the look they anticipated on Aurelius's face when he ran into a hornets' nest of opposition upon landing in Rome. But unknown to Antonius, Publius had been too on edge to follow the plan and wait for him, going ahead to handle the matter himself. He'd thought the better plan was to trap Aurelius in front of the veterans, after he had failed to disclose all to them.

Antonius found Publius slumped, squatting in a corner, sulking like a small child, almost in tears.

"What gives? Are those men I see rushing across the yard the veterans we were waiting to see? Why did you not alert me that they had arrived?"

"I don't know," Publius cried in confusion. "The voices in my head kept telling me that I could trust only myself to give them the message about Aurelius. They said that you were not hard enough, tough enough; that I must believe in myself. That I am the leader of this resistance to Aurelius, not you." Then he sobbed, pitying himself, mumbling repeatedly, "They didn't believe me…they didn't believe me. I told them, and they didn't believe me."

"Come to your senses!" Antonius said, roughly. "Let this be a lesson to you. When we make a plan, keep to it. There will be another time and place, perhaps on this trip, perhaps in Rome, to set something up against Aurelius. We play different roles, you and I. That doesn't mean you're not the leader. This whole resistance is your idea. I accept that. But if a soldier fails to follow plans—well, he usually dies. I'm glad this wasn't a battlefield." Then, pulling himself together, he looked around to be sure no one was watching, hearing their exchange.

"Come on, my friend. Let's go and wait for another day. I don't know what you told them, but at the speed at which they departed, they appeared to be in a huff—angry. What did happen?"

Publius told him that he'd listened to the meeting between Aurelius and them to gather intelligence, and what he'd heard. He described how Aurelius had dealt with them, craftily, not disclosing his true beliefs or his true relationship with Ignatius, and that he couldn't take the cuteness anymore and burst into the meeting to set matters straight.

"No wonder you got the reaction you did. These men, these veterans, are used to a professional hierarchical structure. No matter how loudly you would have shouted, 'Aurelius is a Christian,' they would not have heard you unless you followed military protocol. Come along," Antonius said, putting his arm around Publius's shoulder, "Let's get with the others. We will tell neither of them what happened. We have to hold their confidence. Yes? Okay?"

"Yes. My deep regrets, Antonius," Publius said, straightening his back and stretching himself to as full a height as he could, restoring his prideful, confident face. "I will hold my peace and fight the voices. I promise. I promise. I promise," he said, as if trying to convince himself more than Antonius.

An out-of-control bull! Antonius thought to himself, ruefully. *If Publius does not listen, though our plan to undo Aurelius and those standing in association with him succeed, we might not survive that success.*

Publius was finding out that bravery alone might not be enough to win a battle. When the battle depends on subtle persuasion, hate, for all its power to obsess, might get in its own way, causing the battle to be lost. He had been on the right path the night he bumped into Aurelius and Marius at that barracks doorway when he'd played nice with them, but he'd slipped off of it today. "Never again! Never again!" he vowed.

In my room alone, I cried, making a vow to myself.

The meeting with the veterans had proved me unready to be a representative of Jesus, let alone a martyr, willing to die for Him as was Ignatius. Yes, I'd answered all of the veterans' questions truthfully—viewing the questions discreetly. Yet, I'd not owned up to my friendship with Ignatius or Jesus. I did not defended Christianity. In fact, I practically disavowed it. I used my position as Publius's superior to save myself from being found out a believer, barking orders to distract the veterans from the truth of Publius's assertions. I thought I could be like Ignatius: fearless when the time for truth came. But I could not. Weeping grievously, as one in deep affliction, praying for forgiveness, I continued in this throughout the night, until my tears and pleadings to God were spent.

I arose from my knees, my face tear streaked and my blouse wet from tears and sweat. Then, I declared: "Never again! Never again! God, give me the strength to never deny You again!"

With my burdens lifting, as the sunlight of a new morning, I drifted off to sleep, feeling as if I had splashed my face with warm water, starting a new day, resting in what I knew was the forgiveness of Jesus.

CHAPTER 12
PASSING WINTER'S TESTS

*"My beloved spake, and said unto me, Rise up, my
love, my fair one, and come away. For, lo, the winter
is past..."*
—*Solomon's Song 2:10–11 (KJV)*

In a few days, as I had promised Lucius and his friends, I led my men
out of Philippi, destined for Thessalonica. Of Neapolis, Philippi,
and Thessalonica, Thessalonica's residents were by far the wealthiest.
Perhaps its strategic location explained its wealth. It was situated not
only on the Via Egnata, but also within relatively easy access to two
sea routes, the Aegean Sea to its south and the Adriatic Sea to its west,
both leading to the Mediterranean Sea. This siting made it a center
of trade activity, including an active market where slaves were bought
and sold. Thessalonica was politically important to Macedonia as
well, serving as the seat of the governor for the entire province.

Thessalonica also thrived as a cultural center, where poets, philosophers, and rhetors came to teach and exchange with cultivated,
even sophisticated audiences. Many open-air performances took place
in its amphitheatre, beautifully located on a natural slope between
Mount Khortiatis and the Thermaic Gulf. Thessalonica's grecism
was unmistakable, as its gross dedication to pagan gods showed. The
Roman gods, stepchildren of the Greek gods, were well represented
there as well, including a Roman forum and temples of Serapis, god
of the underworld, and Isis, adopted from the Egyptians, goddess of
fertility.

Buildings for the leisure of its wealthy inhabitants and guests abounded—a large gymnasium, baths, a nympheum, and a hippodrome, all public facilities paid for by levies on trade and commercial activities.

Neither I nor any of my men had seen such an impressive city before. "How could Rome be more magnificent," we asked each other. Our imaginations could not grasp an answer to that question.

In all its splendor, I would find that wintering in Thessalonica, while providing a playground for my men, would prove uncomfortable for Ignatius and me. For, unbeknownst to me when I planned it as a place to spend a peaceful winter, Thessalonica was home to many wealthy and vocal Jews, greatly hostile to the Christians living there. Too late, I learned that I'd traded out a military veteran's problem in Phillipi for a far more incendiary, longstanding and, in the case at hand, a particularly localized problem between Christians and Jews.

Thessalonica had been the site, around AD 50, of a nasty incident when St. Paul preached there in the synagogue. His arrival in Thessalonica followed on the heels of Roman Emperor Claudius's expulsion in AD 49 of all Jews from Rome, due to riots incited by a small group of zealous Jews, advocating revolution against Rome over the installation of a new king. Many of those exiled Jews settled in Thessalonica. Arriving there a year later, Paul found the Jews in no mood to tolerate his presence. Paul's preaching converted some Jews to Christianity, causing divisions in the Jew's ranks. Fearing that open strife would ensue between those thus divided, the Jews worried that undesired commotion might bring unwanted attention to their community. This torturous thought process propelled Jewish leaders to raise a mob to set upon Paul and Christians worshipping at the home of one Jason. But, not finding Paul and the Christians there, the mob dragged Jason to the authorities, in effect blaming the Christians as the true cause of the insurrection in Rome, crying out to the rulers of the city, "These who have turned the world upside down have come here, too. Jason has harbored them, and these are all acting contrary to the decrees of Caesar, saying there is another King—Jesus."

A goodly number of the Jews who Ignatius, I, and my troops would encounter in Thessalonica descended from this strain of Jews who had stirred up trouble against Christians in Paul's day. For years, their ancestors had crammed their minds with tales of their expulsion by Roman authorities, establishing in this passed-on folklore that the Christians, not radical, overly zealous Jews, were the true culprits in causing it. Thus, the Jews of Thessalonica harbored severe prejudices against Christians.

In December, a few months after my men and I settled in Thessalonica, word reached Eli, chief priest of the Jews of Thessalonica, of our presence. Initially, Eli was overjoyed at the plight of Ignatius, happy that the emperor was finally beginning to come down hard on Christians. Yet, when he heard that Ignatius was preaching and teaching in the community, he went on an unholy rampage. Finding that Ignatius was in his city exhorting Christ, in a reprise of the words of his ancestors, he shouted out, "Who brings this acrimony to our place, disrupting the tranquility we enjoy, sowing seeds of condemnation to we who live here without quarrel? We do not wish to be painted with the broad brush of these troublemakers!"

Thus, Eli sent a messenger, Rueben, to see me, seeking to arrange a meeting with me and an assembly of Jews.

———•———

"Welcome, Rueben. It is my great pleasure to meet you," I began, amiably, trying not to show agitation.

"The pleasure belongs to me, Captain Aurelius. I can see from the decorations on your uniform that you have celebrated many victories for Rome. Though Jews, most of us are citizens of Rome. I certainly am one of them," he chuckled.

"We celebrate the generosity of the Empire to our people and us through our support for it. We have interests in the State of Rome that align with yours. Oh, forgive me, Captain, I should have started out welcoming you to our city, asking after your men's welfare here and whether you are enjoying our wonderful comforts," Rueben, taking ownership of the city, boldly declared.

"Oh, yes. The men are having a good time here, sometimes I fear too good a time. The comforts in Thessalonica seem boundless for one desiring to indulge in them. I try to keep my head level and my senses alert, so I abstain from most of the city's comforts—or pleasures. But, yes. This is a spectacular city."

"Then, you are as we are, Captain—you a man of restraint, and we Jews, are, men of restraint. We choose to live peaceably, not riotously, to respect Thessalonica as we do our very places of abode with our families. And who does not crave a peaceable household, Captain?" a cheerily smiling, rotund Reuben concluded.

This Rueben, I thought, *spews words encased in honey, but I feel he conceals a narcissistic spirit. He bears careful listening to. I will call Marius to help me fathom this character.*

"Young soldier! Fetch my man Marius," I ordered a soldier loaned to me from the local command. Ask him to come quickly to meet Reuben and to sit with us."

Reuben, thinking things were starting out smoothly, was taken aback.

"Oh, did I say something that warrants the need for a call up of reinforcements?" he smiled, more engagingly than before.

"Not at all, Reuben. Marius is my right hand. I depend heavily on his advice and help through important discussions and meetings. Yours is such a meeting."

"Oh. I see, Captain. You are quite the diplomat. No wonder you are granted this command," Reuben returned the flattery.

"Then, it is as diplomat to diplomat that we speak, Reuben."

Marius rushed in. "Hello, sir. You summoned me?"

"Yes, Marius. Meet Reuben, representative of Eli, the high priest of the synagogue of the Jews in Thessalonica."

Reuben bowed his head in greeting. Marius could tell by my tone and gestures that I'd brought him into the meeting to help me parry this Reuben into submission. He looked forward to it. Saying he was a high Jewish leader could only mean one thing…that he'd come bearing daggers for Ignatius.

"Marius is a dedicated and committed soldier, as am I. Now, we are ready to proceed."

"Well, I feel at a great disadvantage in the presence of you two powerful forces. I may not be outweighed, but I feel outmanned," he tried joking.

"Just the opposite," Marius said. "As a Roman citizen, which I take you to be, it is my duty to serve and protect you, in war and peace. So, read my presence and that of Captain Aurelius as a double commitment to serve and protect, rather than an effort at double intimidation."

"Oh, I like that! Now, Captain, I see, too, why you brought him in here. Quite clever, Marius."

Marius nodded acceptance of the compliment. Reuben continued, "Eli seeks a meeting between you, or the two of you, and some of our leaders to work toward averting what he perceives as clear omens of danger. You see, there are Christians among us who seem rabid in their adoration of your prisoner, Ignatius. In fact, he is such an interesting and charismatic man that even some in our sect have shown interest. His orations on this Jesus stir controversy—though let me quickly add that we believe that Jesus is merely a contrived, invented, foreign god. A good prophet, at best. And then, to continue, philosophers, seeking to understand any new doctrine, sit in circles with him discussing Jesus, inadvertently giving unintended credence to these atheist teachings."

"May I ask, of the things you have just said, wherein lurks the danger for the state against which you enlist our help?" I implored.

"Well...err...err...well, I am getting to that. I think it should be quite clear, though. As you may have been able to see as you have come to know something of the life of this city, we all live together, all cultures and religions, in peace. The headquartering of the governor of the Macedonian province here demands this environment. We Jews pay our levies like every other Roman, save for a few veterans who are understandably exempt. The Christians and the Jews avoid dealing with each other. I, in fact, look the other way when I pass a known Christian. But, generally there is no strife between us—none that is open, anyway. Yet, this Ignatius, when he speaks to Christians, he brings to their minds the sharp differences in their beliefs and the tenets of Judaism...and between their beliefs and those of the gods of Rome—your gods and the gods of your army, yes, of your civilization. We know that differences exist, but they should not be pointed out at every turn, every meeting, and become open, festering wounds. Can you see what I mean? What our concerns are?"

"Has Ignatius, to your knowledge, called on Christians to cause open strife, some sort of insurrection, against the government of Thessalonica or of Rome?" Marius asked.

"Well... I...I don't see that as the issue. He points out differences in his beliefs and all others. He tells the Jews, the gentiles, the Romans, anyone within hearing of his words, that they are lost forever to a fiery underworld of eternal punishment unless they believe as he does. Wouldn't that be enough to make anyone so accused angry enough...angry enough to defend themselves and their way of life against such...such...blasphemy? That anger, that sort of anger could boil over into mob action against the Christians and Ignatius, and who knows what might happen then. Eli believes it could result in open fighting in the streets of Thessalonica. That sort of thing should not be a part of these modern times. Am I making myself clear, now? Can you see what I mean?"

"Do you not believe that the Jesus of which Ignatius speaks is a mere supernatural apparition, powerless to affect the lives of men?" I asked.

"Yes. At most. That is what we preach in the synagogue. But..."

"Then, why would you worry about such things that you believe are not real? Why would any devout Jew, grounded in his faith, be moved by such?" Marius asked.

"Few are. To be sure, very few are. But the teachings of Ignatius are odious and wrong," Reuben stiffened his protest.

"But if few of the Jews believe in Jesus, then your people are suffering no meaningful divisions. And I would suppose that such as are persuaded by Ignatius, surely your doctrine can recapture?" Marius continued.

"Gentlemen. May I confide in you? Reuben asked, whispering curiously.

"Yes, of course," I responded, musing as to what would come next.

"For those few Jews who have left the synagogue and become Christians, it seems that some peculiar spell possesses them. They become immovable in their resolve to stay with the Christians. None have returned to us. Not one. This magic that those of the ilk of Ignatius work on these few Jews, and on many others besides, makes men lose their natural senses. We Jews choose to live separate lives from the rest of the world to safeguard our traditions and to live unobtrusively in society. But these Christians live separate from the world to establish a new kingdom, not of this society. Is this not a threat to Rome—a threat to you? Is this not a threat we should work on together to avert?"

"Do these Christians have an army to bring against that of Rome? An army that can overrun us and establish this new kingdom of Jesus, which you say is in opposition to Rome?" I asked.

"Now you confuse me, Captain. Are we in a debating club here?"

"Perhaps, of a sort. For my mission has one purpose—to deliver Ignatius to Rome alive for execution. Emperor Trajan assigned this mission. I have seen the streets of this city, and they are filled with soldiers and armaments. I am certain that these forces can stand up to any group of Christians that could be raised to replace the government of Rome with that of Jesus. If there is any doubt about that, then it is to the governor of this province and its military leaders to whom you should take that evidence—evidence of the threats of insurrections. My small contingent has no part to play in securing this vast Thessalonica territory.

Furthermore, insofar as Ignatius's exhortations of Christians to remain faithful to their religion and his proselytizing for all to join him and fellow Christians, I have witnessed this sort of thing in every city in which we have encamped along the way, from Antioch, through Tarsus, Smyrna, Troas, Neapolis, Philippi, and others, and no disturbance of the peace has come out of it. Therefore, I, having seen the lack of a threat materializing in these places, would doubt that it would be any different here."

Rueben looked as if he felt himself under attack.

Then, narrowing my eyes, I concluded, "Unless, what is different here is that some may raise a mob to attack Ignatius or his Christian followers while they meet with him in Thessalonica. That would be different. That would lead to unrest. And that would implicate the success of our mission and cause us to repel any such mob. And, sir, it would also cause us to ferret out the source of the disorder that threatened our prisoner, in order that we might answer to the emperor for his loss—that is to say before our own executions. To do this ferreting out, we would enlist any of the good soldiers of Thessalonica as might help us to see that Emperor Trajan's execution order for Ignatius is carried out by him, not by someone, some mob, in Thessalonica. Now, do you understand what I mean?"

Reuben batted his eyes, clearing them to make sure that the look in my eyes matched the unmistakable feel of contempt in my voice. He looked as if he felt sorely intimidated, but he tried to recover.

"I think I may understand you. I will report to Eli that you perceive no danger to Rome of... Ignatius's...meetings. And that if... as you intimate...if an insurrection breaks out against Ignatius and the Christians and a local group...a mob, as you say, that he has your assurance that you will devote all of your resources to root out...to root out the cause of it...and make sure that the peace of our community is not long disturbed...if disturbed at all," Reuben haltingly summed up, sweating profusely.

"Then, I believe that will conclude our meeting, unless of course, you have further questions."

"No, Captain. You have answered all my questions...completely. Thank you. With your permission, I will take my leave."

"Yes. Of course. Thank you for coming. Please give my best to your high priest, Eli, and tell him that I hope he remains in good health."

"I will. Good meeting both of you."

Reuben gathered up his huge toga, wrapping it around his very wide body. He called for an assistant. Grabbing on to his aide's arm, he attempted an awkward genuflect, then turned and walked slowly away, saying, when he mistakenly thought he'd moved a safe distance from our hearing, under his breath, "What a waste."

Once he left, Marius and I celebrated, laughing.

"Did you see the look on his face? He had no idea where we were going, what our questions sought to uncover," Marius exclaimed.

"Yes Marius. He felt the chill of winter early, I suspect. But he deserved a little shock out of his smug comfort zone."

"Well, he got it. I guess we will soon see how well he carried our message to his high priest."

A few hours later, Rueben made his report to Eli.

Eli was not amused at Reuben's report.

"And he plans for us to endure these insults, these assaults against us through the winter? Nonsense! I will see that the proper authorities hear us on this!" Eli fumed. "We have friends among those in high position here, including Governor Balbinus. We are taxpayers; they are not. We'll see who will need protection from whom in the end."

Reuben just stared. Eli had not seen Aurelius's look.

•————•————•

Nonplused by Eli's predictions of doomsday riots in the streets, were Ignatius not muzzled, Governor Balbinus shook his head, himself despairing over wasted time.

"For the life of me, Eli, you worry as an old lady over a tear in her undergarments, should a stranger attempt to peek beneath her clothing. Not that her modesty is any less compromised or worthy of protection as that of the most striking young virgin in the land. It's just that the chance of someone attempting to peek thereunder is as far removed as the days of her youth," he exclaimed, at which all of his loyalist, sitting around him for this meeting, joined in sustained guffaws.

"Governor. This is serious. These Christians are a nuisance when aroused to fanaticism. They can be stubborn, and...and... atheist...and anarchist. This Ignatius is not going to his death in Rome quietly. Thessalonica, I hear, is the last stop overland before he is taken by sea to Rome. Escaping at sea is near impossible. If he is to be freed by his followers, it will happen here...in your place...

under your jurisdiction. I feel confident that he would like nothing better than to take a few of us to your underworld with him as he goes. He's a desperate man with nothing to lose, Governor. Who is more desperate…and…more dangerous than a criminal condemned to death? As a citizen of Rome, I…"

"Citizens of Rome are we all, Eli," the governor said dryly. "Distinguish yourself in some other way and, while you are at that, distinguish your petition as well. To me, it sounds like the several false alarms you have set before me over the years. You are the spinner of dire omens. One of my men coined that on your last stop here. I don't remember which of you coined that, but remind me to put a few coins in your pay this quarter, for it was thoroughly clever." More laughter.

"But I digress, Eli. This threat, I believe, like the others, exists only in your overactive imagination. So, let me ask you to imagine this. Suppose I say I will arrest Ignatius and throw him in prison. Would that appease you, address your fears?"

"Why, most certainly!" Eli answered, delight springing in his voice. "I would urge you to do that, for then he would be silenced and out of sight so long as he is here."

"Seriously? Throw him in jail when he is already condemned to die? Take him out of the hands of the soldiers who guard him under direct orders of Emperor Trajan himself? And would you propose that we do this by force, because I cannot imagine that the soldiers who guard him would surrender him to me, at the risk of their own deaths—because, as you may know Eli, under Roman law, if a prisoner escapes custody, the custodian is executed. Following this logic further, why should my office and my men take on so hot a prisoner, who others want to break free, and risk his escape while he is in my hands, with me then facing a new and I believe an unwarranted threat to my own life…and…of course, to those of my men," Balbinus said, catching himself at the last minute to assuage the sensibilities of his men by including them in his risk assessment. But, by now, he'd grown tired of accommodating Eli. He didn't see the point in asking more questions to which he knew Eli had no sensible or useful reply.

Eli could tell that his talk with the governor was probably doing more harm than good, implicating the betrayal by him of the great survival principle of Jews under Roman rule: Stay to yourself and hope that you go unnoticed and undisturbed by the government and, when asked, feign unshakeable loyalty to the state and especially to the emperor, or in this case, the governor, avoiding annoying them at all cost. He thanked Governor Balbinus and bowed out of the meeting.

From the time of that meeting, the wintering of Aurelius and his men and Ignatius went well and uneventfully. Publius and Antonius quietly plotted for a showdown in Rome, and strengthened their relationship with Decimus, Ruffinus, Minucius, Quintas and, now, Dentatus, the men in their camp. They had thought of connecting with the Jews to foment trouble for Ignatius and the Christians, but in the dead of winter, they felt more like seeking the certainty of warmth offered by the wine and women of Thessalonica than like doing the hard work of managing a conspiracy with Eli, Reuben, and other fickle Jewish leaders, with whom they met, but by whom they were not impressed.

December turned to January, January to February, and when February pointed toward March, the snows started melting away. The undeniable signs of spring, sprouting trees, singing wrens, and bursting flower buds noticed me of our time to depart Eli's city. The winter was past. I was happy about that. Now I had to face the spring and move on to Rome. Rome, the Imperial City—the center of power and treachery. I could not know what lay ahead there, but, I no longer feared it.

CHAPTER 13
NEARING THE JOURNEY'S END

*"Thus saith the Lord, which maketh a way in the
sea, and a path in the mighty waters...remember ye
not the former things, neither consider the things of
old. Behold, I will do a new thing."*
　　　　　　　　　　　—Isaiah 43:16, 18–19 (KJV)

Back in heavy chains, Ignatius knelt down to pray on the shore of
the Aegean Sea before boarding a merchant ship bound for Corinth.
Annoyed by the delay occasioned by his praying, Publius and
Antonius sought to claim that his dallying flowed from his realiza-
tion that he was in the final stretch of his death march to Rome.

"Come on, old man," Publius scowled. "You've had your wrists
and ankles freed long enough that now you should be able to walk
with as spry a gait as a young stag. Oh, I see," he mocked, "you have
not fallen down at all. You deliberately got down on your knees, did
you? Well, good thing you did, for I have greatly missed jerking you
along by your chains, forcing a fall here and there. But do I divine
something different, something even more sinister happening here?
For all your vaunted fearlessness, are you flinching before your god as
we draw yet closer to your door of death? Rise. Let us move on before
your reticence delays our departure."

Ignatius ignored Publius's taunts. He might have been too
transfixed on the things of God to hear him. But I heard.

"He will be allowed to pray. I doubt that he prays for his relief,
but for our safe voyage, and that of the master and crew of this ship.

By all events, it is my call whether we board today or tomorrow. Let him pray in peace—without your interference!" I ordered.

Boarding the ship, we all quickly wished we had taken another vessel, for this one reeked with the stench of death. It had made the long trek from Carthage to Thessalonica, loaded with ivory and the human cargo of African slaves, bound for the trading blocks, to feed the lusts for wealth and the decadent habits for pleasure of the people of Thessalonica. Although the Christian church was strong there and had become the hub of the spread of the Gospel in Macedonia and Greece, Christians made up only a small part of its population of around two hundred thousand, and its effects on the ethos of the lives of the people there was still just emerging. Thus, this ship, apparently now clean of the bodies and waste of the African slaves who did not survive the voyage to Thessalonica and the human waste in which survivors and those lost alike were forced to wallow during their sordid passage, had been unable to shed its oppressive odor, despite thorough scrubbings by its crew and some land dwellers. Even with the ship's tall and impressive sails, its solid outfitting, its cavernous size, and its splendid carved construction, the eerie and silent cries of its sacrificed innocents, Ignatius later told me, revealed themselves through his spirit before he set foot on the ship. Perhaps that was why he instantly knelt and prayed at its gangplank, to cast out its demons and to ward off evil spirits. I hoped the demons had fled, but if they did they didn't take with them the stench from the ship's awful work.

The voyage of a little over four hundred miles to Corinth took less than two days. It would have been shorter, had the travel been in open seas, for the winds were adequate and friendly. But the many beautiful islands lying throughout the Aegean Sea, together forming the Grecian Archipelago, somewhat slowed the navigational pace. No one complained, however, as the ship's master acted as a tour guide, helping to show off God's marvelous creations. These breathtaking islands, some made from volcanic lava and some of pure marble, captivated all its passengers, almost drowning the differences between them. Some of the scattered islands in the northern Aegean Sea, where our ship entered the waters, the master explained, inspired

Greek legends and mythology, out of which many of the gods of Rome later emerged.

"How could men see the beauty of the universe and not realize the handiwork of the Almighty?" Ignatius shouted. "As King David proclaimed, 'The heavens declare the glory of God. And, the firmament his handiwork. How much less these magnificent seas and isles?"

He'd taught us that the world was not yet idyllic and would not be so until the second coming of Christ. This thought set my heart rejoicing, even as the throngs of lost men around us, traveling with us, were giving praise to Neptune, god of the sea, in their pagan tradition. That Rome sought to punish Ignatius for trying to bring them to the knowledge of Jesus did not mute his mood. I despaired as Ignatius continued to cry out to God at the thought of all the men who would be lost forever because they would not believe and accept the free gift of salvation.

"You are without excuse," Ignatius cried out, "these awesome creations reveal God's goodness and glorious handi-works. See Him for what He is, the Creator of all things in the universe, seen and unseen. Do not suppress the reality of all powerful God. Recognize and worship Him. You are without excuse!"

"Shut him up!" some called out to me, but I drew protectively close to him and stared hard at them. The shouting quieted.

In Corinth, to our great relief, we boarded a ship that had traveled there from Alexandria. It brought papyrus, drugs, spices, perfumes, and corn as its cargo, and with that the smells of life. Unloading some of that cargo in Corinth, the ship picked up bronze and marble, beautiful but scentless, and added the sweet aroma of honey, forever exchanging the opprobrious smells of death for these delicious ones, eliminating the old ones from the minds of us travelers, eager to forget them.

This sunnier environment did not arrest the dark voices and sick thoughts that daily racked Publius's head. They arose in him every day of the five-day voyage from Corinth to Puteoli, Italy. He fought the urgings night and day, as they kept telling him to make Aurelius and Ignatius "disappear" over the side of the ship, never to be heard from again. Indeed, when the ship stopped briefly in

Messina, Sicily, the voices were so loud and powerful that Publius had to leave the ship for the twelve hours it docked there, in order to turn his thoughts away from the ship and the venal opportunity the ship seemed to continually give him to contemplate murder at sea.

In the early morning of the sixth day of our disembarkation from Corinth, our ship pulled into the harbor at Puteoli. My heart fluttered upon waking and I bounded up to make my rounds, my gait lithe and agile, checking on my men and the condition of Ignatius.

"Thank You, Jesus, for delivering me thus far on this journey You have chosen for me. A life with You is nearer than ever. Continue to give me the strength to bear Your cross. I gladly bear it," I heard Ignatius pray.

Decimus and Otho, who were chained to him, shook their heads in disbelief, but obviously for different reasons.

Leaving the ship to get my bearings on the dock and locate the soldiers who were to meet us there, I saw another ship from Carthage unloading. It sagged under the heavy weight of African slaves, much as I imagined the one we boarded in Thessalonica had. I saw a big cat, a leopard from Africa, prowling in its pen, and reflected on Ignatius's characterization of our troop. This dangerous, solitary hunter, with his mysterious spots—spots which did not change from cub to adult, from life to death. He did not roar like a lion; he did not growl intimidatingly, true to the stealth required of a silent night killer. What did it all mean?

Then, my heart stopped, as I also saw at least ten pens of African lions, all males, with thick, imposing manes, growling at all who passed. I could not help but wonder if among them was the lion that would taste the precious blood of Ignatius. And I wondered also whether the African slaves on board would be sacrificed at the lion's teeth as well for the entertainment of Emperor Trajan and the elite of Rome. I realized, in the case of Ignatius, that he would be escorted by these lions to a glorious life with Jesus, but I wondered about the others who would die, both needlessly and unprofitably, and my heart ached thinking of the cruelty of it all.

A hundred miles away, at the end of the Appian Way on which we were about to travel, we would finally reach Rome. I located the soldiers greeting us, who carried with them fresh horses, wagons, chariots, and supplies for us. The trip would take another five days.

As we moved out, thoughts of the many talks and plans my father and I had made about our one day traveling to Rome together rushed into my mind. We said we would visit as father and son—proud sons of the Roman Empire. He whetted my appetite to reach Rome as he'd regaled me with his experiences there—his indulgences in all of its attractions—including his hope that we would visit its holy temples. I felt a certain emptiness in my soul in the place where my father's continual presence had always been, and momentarily could not arrest the sorrow that surged in me. Yet, I felt no desire for the pleasures of Rome as I had planned before. Though I felt no regret for the cause of our separation, I still missed my father terribly. My only true sorrow, deep down, was that I was unable to share the joy of my new faith with him. Whatever sacrifice I might make in Rome, if it caused him to believe, then it would be more than worth it. I comforted myself with this final thought, and it set me at peace.

I looked back at Ignatius. He was beaming, riding in a wagon just behind my chariot. He smiled at me, and I at him.

"To Rome," I shouted the roaring command. "To Rome!" my men responded in unison. And those others traveling the Appian Way with us joined in our shouting. "To Rome! To Rome! To Rome!" they cried back with one voice.

All that we had gone through together in the past year between Ignatius and me, and everything each of us had experienced in our lives before this moment, we now, happily, voluntarily, left all of it behind.

When the other voices died down, I heard a single cry from just to the rear of me.

"To Rome!" Ignatius shouted in a loud voice. "To Rome!"

The hair stood up on the nape of my neck.

Indeed, we had come a long way over land and sea, overcoming the stifling limitations of fear, tradition, family ties, and earthly ambitions, leaving it all behind us for God's expansive and liberating new thing.

CHAPTER 14
PREPARING TO WIN

"Likewise also was not Rahab the harlot justified by works, when she had received the messengers, and had sent them out another way?"
—James 2:25 (KJV)

The Appian Way led directly through the Porta Appia, one of the gateways into Rome. Converging smartly with the Via Latina, it became one of two roads delivering traffic to the front door of a huge bathhouse, the Bath of Caracalla. This spectacle of the pagan world, unlike many smaller bathhouses, featured not just hot and cold baths but also large lecture halls, conversation rooms, swimming pools, dressing rooms, and gardens. One could exercise, read, get a massage, and listen to and interact with philosophers or poets there. With baths for men and men and for men and women in close proximity, public nudity in that, as well as in some other bathhouses, was not frowned upon. To most Romans, bathhouses, along with the other principal entertainments—dangerous circus chariot racing, blood-dripping arenas, and lewd theater performances—represented the best in life's pleasures. But to Christians, they were the picture of immorality and debauchery.

I could only imagine the pain it caused Ignatius as he passed the Bath of Caracalla and saw the large flow of well-dressed patrons going in and out of it. It had to mightily assault his sensibilities. His heart would have sagged even more, had he known that the huge building we neared next was the Circus Maximus, for he would have reflected on those who had suffered purposeless deaths and maiming there in brutal chariot races and death battles of slaves or gladiators, sometimes pitting slaves or performers against wild beasts, to the delight and for the entertainment of Rome's most prosperous citizens. Sometimes these circus events boasted as many as 255,000 people in attendance. Looking to his left, though Ignatius had no way to know it as we continued our entry, behind Capitoline Hill, one of the seven hills on which Rome was built, stood the infamous Mamertime Prison, the place where Peter and Paul were held fifty years earlier before their executions. And if these sights would have caused him despair, those coming up on our right would have broken his heart and raised his ire in equal measures, for there, row upon row, and rows deep, stood a world of gleaming white temples to the various Roman gods, temples of marble, gold, and precious stones, bearing masterfully done drawings and etchings, the centerpieces being temples to Jupiter and Juno, these two with columns so tall as to seem to enter the clouds. The world's most famous fora were also there, including the Forum of Caesar and the Forum of Trajan. Trajan's Temple and those of other deified emperors, bearing their god-like images, also rose against the skyline.

Had he been able to see far to his right past these temples, just east of Equiline Hill, he would have seen the cavernous "Roman Coliseum," a monstrosity of a building, a miracle of architecture and engineering, and the place that featured great military exhibitions— parades and reenactments of land and sea victories—as well as other bloody battles between men and beasts. In less than thirty minutes in Rome, Ignatius, wittingly or not, passed both the places that represented the cause of the ordering of his execution, the temples of the gods of Rome and its deified emperor, and the place where it was to be carried out, the world-renowned Roman Coliseum.

Surrounding it all, in all of its staggering dimensions, stretching for miles in either direction, touching every horizon in sight, lay Rome, the largest and best-known city and the most important seat of government in the entire civilized world, terribly beautiful and terribly ugly. Its crowded side streets, now also bulging with throngs of visitors, in Rome for Trajan's military festivities, teemed with markets and shops, its multiple-story tenements filled to capacity. Its base squalor amidst its ungodly wealth was equally mind bending. Marius and I struggled to comprehend it all.

"Well, we are here, Marius—Rome. The Imperial City. Can you believe this place?" I exclaimed, bubbly.

"It is incredible, Aurelius. I can see that Thessalonica is no match for it, even though we have just arrived. I have dreamt of the day that I would see Rome, but I could never have imagined that it would be under the present circumstances."

"I know. I know," I said, quietly. "It's bittersweet. But, even so, there is no denying that Rome shouts loudly to the world, *I'm bigger than you! I'm better than you!* For better or worse, we are a part of it, and it of us, and that induces a certain pride in one's innards. It does in mine. It makes me want to hope for it."

"I wish I could see how great our God is, Aurelius, you know, touch and see Him as a man can touch and see Rome."

"Ignatius says we will. But not today and not in this life. I feel in my spirit that one day we will. One day the whole world will bow down before Him," I added blissfully.

The seat of Rome's government, the place where its emperor, its senate, and its tribunes, counselors, and magistrates met to do Rome's business, sat parallel to the fora, a fitting positioning, since the State of Rome controlled religion. Many of its priests performing sacrifices and conducting ceremonies to win the favor of the gods, were government officials, appointed or elected to office. Emperor Trajan himself held the highest position in the state's religion, pontifex maximus. The merger between the state and its many, nonexclusive gods was complete. Protecting the state, necessarily, then, meant protecting its gods.

The soldiers who met my troop at Porta Appia were members of the Praetorian guard, a cohort of personal body guards for military leaders and officials. Emperor Trajan commanded this guard personally, and its Praetorian Prefect, Macennius, served directly under Trajan and had day-by-day operational control of this more than 5,500-strong force. Of this number, about 500 were personal body guards for Trajan. Fierce loyalty was demanded of this guard, so fierce that while the majority of the Roman Army was no longer made up of Italians, every man serving in the guard was of Italian descent. As my men and I passed the various government buildings, the presence of a large number of armed soldiers, not in uniforms but in white tunics, their heads covered, the unmistakable dress of the Praetorian guard, definitely signaled that Emperor Trajan was in one of them. With that observation, a huge lump filled my throat. I figured I would probably soon be in Trajan's presence, reporting on his mission. Though I felt prepared to deal with however things went, I anticipated a struggle that, if it went poorly, could make me pray as Christ had prayed in Gethsemane, that that cup might pass.

My orders were to meet Macennius at the barracks of the Praetorian Guard building, far in the northeast boundary of the city. When we finally arrived there in the midafternoon, Macennius's men summoned him outside his barracks to greet us. I had met him years earlier in the company of my father.

"By Mercury, Aurelius, you have traveled well, reaching us on schedule, your prisoner secure. I never doubted it, nor did Emperor Trajan. Come in at once. My men will take charge of this Ignatius. Atilius! Reminius! Take Aurelius's men's horses and stable them and show his men to the quarters to which each is assigned. There are fresh tunics on the beds and hot baths waiting. Make sure you match the tunics with the men—for I see that a few are very tall, one is tall and fat, and one is short and stout." Macennius's men laughed. All of my men laughed, too, except Publius.

"Lock the prisoner in the dungeon. We don't want to lose him after all the trouble these men went through to get him here."

They took hold of Ignatius, treating him roughly. I stared at Ignatius, my heart going out to him.

"Aurelius, come with me. Let's have a drink, discuss, and plan. Are you okay? Where is your usual gregariousness?" Macennius chided.

"Let's go inside as you say, sir. We are all tired and will require some rest, as you can understand. If it's okay with you, we can swap a few tales about the old Legio X, which you served in with my father when I was a cub, a little later. Maybe I'll be better company tomorrow. But this was a generous reception. I'm deeply grateful," I said haltingly.

"Of course. Of course, you are tired."

Then, Macennius shouted to one of his slaves, "Get on with it and serve his men with food and drink. Give them massages. Whatever they need to relax."

"Atilius, if any of his men have more life in them than Aurelius, give them a short tour of some of your favorite places in the city. You know what I mean?"

"Now, all you men who are of the Aurelius troop. If Atilius gives you a turn around town, don't try and drink everything in in one night. Take small, small sips, gentlemen, and those of you into biting, small, small bites. There is a lot to consume here and you don't want to get your bellies full the first evening. Easy, men. Easy with them, Atilius, agreed?"

Atilius nodded and laughed with all the others.

The part of the barracks where Macennius lodged and which he offered special guests, was beautifully appointed with hardwood ceilings and bronze fans. The entrance floors were wide and covered with marble. The walls were swirled plaster of orange and red, the colors of the empire, with striking paintings of war scenes and military triumphs. A bronze statue of Emperor Trajan was in the entry hall, and the Roman gods of war and war strategies were prominently displayed. Macennius escorted me into a lounge room with a beautiful walnut table in the center and marble fountains leading to an outdoor garden. The table was covered with various meats, including venison and boar; fruits, including grapes and pomegranates, and choice wines. We sat on red leather couches that were arranged close together in an L shape. Macennius clapped his hands and a beautiful slave girl appeared, bowing before him. He stood to whisper something in her ear, and I noticed that she looked at me after Macennius began whispering and nodded her head. She moved away quickly, purposefully, flashing a halfhearted smile.

"I told her you would need a bath and some relaxation before dinner tonight. I gave her leave to help you wash—to wash your back, to bathe you, to bathe with you—whatever you want. You understand me? Whatever comforts you desire. Maybe just a bath now, if you are really tired, and more later—understand?" Macennius said, smiling, hinting transparently that the girl belonged to me, however I wanted to use her.

I understood something that Macennius did not: the boundaries within which, since my conversion to Christianity, I had chosen—was obligated—to live, the same ones I'd heard Ignatius and his Christian followers talk about when it came to sexual morality. A part of me wished I was my old self again, for the girl was lovely indeed and I had not had a woman in my arms for many months. I also recognized that I was in a tricky spot with Macennius, because I did not want to offend or upset him by refusing his hospitality or to make him think I was acting queerly.

"What I need now is a good bath. Could you please send the slave girl to my quarters…wherever they are in this fantastic place… after she has prepared a bath for me? Then, I…we…can take it from there. Thank you. What is her name?"

"Isabella. She is from Spain, though I think by way of Greece. Oh, I've paid little mind to her background. The point is, her grandmother served the emperor's father when they lived in Spain, and the family followed him to Italy. The mother was to be free and so too this girl, but her father left them in debt to Trajan. Something like that got her here. But why bother with these things? She's beautiful and she is all yours. What more could you ask? Let me show you to your place and I will have Isabella knock on your door soon."

Macennius must have noticed what he assumed was a look of slight embarrassment on my face.

"Now, Aurelius, I know we have not had the type of relationship where we pass girls around. But don't be embarrassed or tight. We are both men. Relax. You are a grown man now, not the boy who knew me as a man with your father years ago. I can tell you this. In our day, your father's and mine, we would have killed for such a night as stands before you. Okay. We are close enough. Right around the corner, the big suite with the door open is yours, as is anything else in this place that you need. An old slave will help you get set up. He stands at your door, waiting for you. See you at supper in about three hours."

As Macennius turned to walk away, I called out to him.

"Commander Macennius, sir. Where is the prisoner held here?"

"Oh, I see. Duty consumes you, preoccupies your thoughts over wine and a beautiful woman? Don't worry about him anymore. He is securely bound and locked away. You have finished your part. Now he is in our hands. I suppose, though, you will want to see the final act—his being fed to the lions—before you depart Rome.

"I will see to it that you get tickets to that finale—tickets so close in that you will feel as if you, yourself, are in the arena."

I shuddered inside.

"Oh, and Emperor Trajan will probably want to thank you for your service. He has told me that he must see you and properly release you from your duties. I would not be surprised at all if he has a special tribute in mind for you. You know that you are one of his favorites—and not just because of the service of your father with him. He's come to respect you personally, on your own account. And who knows if you will not one day replace me here in Rome, as soon as I have the good sense to retire, as has Claudius. Trajan will tell me when he wants to see you, and I will let you know. My best guess is that he will meet with you in five or six days, just before the festivities. But as far as Ignatius goes, don't worry about him. He's going nowhere. He is securely bound and tightly locked down with no chance of escape."

"Thank you, sir." Forcing a smile, I entered my suite and quickly shut the door behind me, letting out a deep sigh. I felt a tear on my cheek, and plucked it away.

I sat down heavily on my bed. My mind drifted to Ignatius. I wanted to see him badly, to see after his welfare.

What did Macennius mean by saying that he was securely bound and tightly locked down, I wondered? Was he bound to a wall on a damp floor in a dark dungeon? Was he being tortured or tormented, maybe even beaten? I suddenly felt that I had to see for myself.

Then another thought crowded my mind: the dread of having dinner with Macennius. The talk would certainly be mostly about my father, old stuff and new questions—what my father and I had done together in the past and what we were doing together now that he was retired. As I was in deep worry about that dinner conversation, a knock came to my door.

"Master, may I come in?"

"Yes, sure. Enter."

"I have your robes and towels. I am here to assist you in bathing, at your pleasure, sir," Isabella said meekly, looking down at her feet.

In the light of the lamps in my room, Isabella looked more stunning than before. Tall and slim, yet curvaceous, her hips widening in the right places, in years past I would have fulfilled my lust with her.

But tonight, lowering my head to look into her large dark eyes, I immediately pitied her.

"Show me to the bathing room," I asked her warmly.

"Yes, sir. Follow me. I have prepared the water for you and have put a fragrance in it that most men like. I will be happy to make it hotter or colder, to your liking—as you desire."

Steam blinded us as we entered the area leading to the deep bathing pool. I took her hand and whispered to her.

"Stay here in this outer area. If anyone asks you if you bathed me or bathed with me and whether I enjoyed it, tell them yes. Understood?"

Isabella's eyes lit up, and she broke into the widest and most beautiful smile.

"I have never been shown kindness by any man, certainly not by any Roman soldier, and absolutely not by a soldier of your high rank, sir," she murmured. Her relief and her gratitude toward me became obvious, and she quickly and happily did as I said. In a short while, I emerged from the bathing pool, a new robe wrapped around me.

"Take the robe I left on the wooden bench and do whatever you normally do with it. Then, go to Macennius and say to him that I said that I so enjoyed your company that I would like to be released from the dinner invitation he extended to me to spend more time with you. I would like to take dinner in my room—the two of us. Tell him that I asked you to bring venison, fish, some cheeses, wine, and grapes that you will feed to me with your hands. Tell him that I want you to dress in some finery to entertain me. He will understand."

She smiled mischievously. "I will. I will gladly."

About twenty minutes later, Isabella returned with some of the meal I had requested, then went back several times with the rest of the food and drink to complete my order.

"Tell me, what did Macennius say when you told him we would take a meal together in my room.

"Now, that's more like it!" he said "That's the son of Claudius!"

We burst into joyous laughter.

Isabella and I had a splendid evening together, eating a delicious meal and drinking wine, locked away from prying eyes. To the outside world, and particularly to Macennius, we were engaged in passionate lovemaking, probably with some erotic massages thrown in here and there. But within that suite, I got acquainted with her in a different way. I inquired about her background, learned about her family, explored her dreams, and asked about what it would take to secure her freedom and whether she earnestly desired it. I asked about her family's debts to Trajan. I told her of my travels and of the things to see in the world.

"Of course, I want to be free, and I will be one day. I am saving a few coins here and there, but it will take years at my pace. However, I am determined and I will get it done," she vowed. "And, I hope someday that I can travel widely, as you have, to see the world and to have a profession of which I can be proud."

We talked, drank, and ate well past the evening and into the early hours of the morning. We also had a good time mocking Macennius and enjoying the trick we were playing on him. Then, as we prepared to quit our night, I asked Isabella a serious question.

"Do you know where the prisoner Ignatius is held? If you do, can you take me there?" I whispered, as if I expected Macennius to be listening at the door.

"Yes," she said eagerly. "He is held in a small dungeon near the slave quarters. I will tell him tonight when I pass, if the chance presents itself, that you asked about him."

"No. You must not. Tomorrow, I want you to take me there. But tonight, you will not return to the slave quarters. Tonight, you will stay here with me and enjoy the comfort of my fine bed. Come."

She happily nodded yes, and climbed into my bed, next to where I sat upon it. I removed myself from beside her, kissed her on the forehead, and lay on the skin of a bear that had been made into a soft rug at the foot of my bed, where I slept soundly.

"You sly fox!" Macennius declared the next morning. "Tired, were you? I was not peeping, but I did notice your lantern light on until near two in the morning. You were pleased with her?"

"Yes. Yes. Very much so! Thank you!"

"Your father had your stamina, or you have his, I guess I should say. And, not to boast, but so did I. Nothing like a good wench to warm a soldier's bed in the crisp springtime."

"She seemed to find comfort in my bed, also," I continued the charade, tongue in cheek.

"Well spoken, Aurelius!" Macennius laughed, slapping me on the back. "A man must have confidence in pleasuring a woman!"

"I would like to see her again, and..."

"You dirty, dirty dog! Of course, you may. She's yours, as I said."

"Please send her to me, then, say, in three hours' time. Is that okay?"

"To feed you again? A lunch treat, perhaps?" he grinned.

"Perhaps, sir."

"Stop calling me sir, Aurelius. We are both officers in the service of the emperor. Though I am old enough to be your father, I do not relish feeling that old. Call me Macennius. And, by the way, tell me, how is my friend Claudius. You have not spoken of him."

"Fat, I hear. I have not seen him in a while, with all my recent duties. He moved to the Arabian Peninsula to an estate there. One of my friends reported to me that his father visited with him several months ago and his health was fine and he was as feisty and hard-headed as ever. I..."

"So," Macennius laughed, mercifully relieving me of the obligation to continue talking about my father, "then nothing has changed except his weight. That is one of the things I worry about—growing old and soft in retirement. That is, I think, my whole fear of retiring, that and losing my position of power, just getting lost with nothing to get up for in the morning. I want to stay fit and hard, defying my gray hair as long as possible. But I do sometimes wonder what living on my own estate, free of the call of any man on my time, would feel like," his said, his thoughts seeming to drift. "But that's a conversation for another day. Good morning," he said, ending the conversation abruptly. I couldn't be sure, but I felt I heard a sad, perhaps a regretful, tone in Macennius's voice, the tone of a man who didn't know how to leave a job in which he knew in his heart he'd stayed on for far too long.

In good spirits, I sought out Marius, finding him sitting on the outside steps of the barracks, looking glum.

"Marius, there you are! How was your evening?"

"I would say quite boring, compared to yours. I did not want to go out carousing with the men, for I felt my new faith did not permit it. So, I ducked the massage parlors and brothels, and especially the harlots. Since I was staying in my quarters, I came over to your room to visit. But at your door I heard the unmistakable sound of female laughter, so I returned to my place and slept alone."

"Well, I cannot say that I slept alone, my friend. But I did not sleep with a woman, either."

"Oh, so that was a man's voice I heard?"

"The slave girl, Isabella, was given to me for a night of pleasure. Being too much of a gentleman and not wanting to appear an ungrateful guest, I did not refuse my host. I did have a night of pleasure with her—pleasurable laughter and good conversation. That was all. I did not know how else to handle Macennius's insistence that I take her to my bath and my bed. But if she came to me pure, then she left this morning unspoiled. Don't fret that. Let's talk about things that matter, like the welfare of Ignatius. Isabella is going to take me where he is being held, or at least show me the way. Will you come with me?"

"Of, course, yes. But why do we go in secret? Why not just ask Macennius if he will permit you to check on him?"

"I asked Macennius about him, but he brushed it off, telling me not to be concerned with him because he is no longer my prisoner, but his. He is right on that score, of course. I can't even see what good I can do by seeing him. But I am worried that he may be suffering unnecessarily."

"I understand. But of course, he is suffering unnecessarily. There is nothing to be done about that. More, there is nothing he would want you to try and do about it. Soon, he will be in a better place. Don't worry about him. My heart is not cold in this. You know that he would tell you just what I have."

Marius was right. I'd lost my perspective because of my love for Ignatius. How could a slave girl take me to see Ignatius undetected? Surely, we would be found out. There could be no secrets in a barracks full of men competent enough to guard Rome's most treasured leaders. Ignatius's fate was sealed. I could no longer loosen his chains nor even offer him a dipper of water.

"We will have to see Trajan, you know. He will honor us, I think, our troop, I mean. He may have a special honor for me, I'm afraid, though I don't deserve it."

"Surely, you would rather that outcome than to get what you deserve," Marius joked. "If Trajan comes bearing gifts, I will gladly accept mine. But who can predict what our emperor will do. This is Rome, and even emperors die at the hands of their friends here. Remember what happened to Julius Caesar."

"I remember. I do."

———————●————————

"Around noon, Macennius sent Isabella to me. She was anxious to speak.

"I saw your prisoner," she said, breathlessly. "He told me to tell you he was, well, satisfied in the hands of the Lord. That he still felt unworthy as a sacrifice, but that he was still praying for more righteousness, more perfection. He said to tell you that he loves you and that God loves you and that he does not want you to chance coming to see about him. What did he mean?"

"What did you say to him? Did you tell him that I planned to have you take me to him? Why would you…"

"No, sir. No, sir. I did not speak a word to him. He told me these things. He called me as I passed by. I did not see him before that. Somehow, he knew these things. Is he a magician?"

"No, Isabella. He's a prophet of God. A Christian, as am I."

"A Christian? You? A soldier? How can that be?" she gasped.

"It was him. He taught me how to be a Christian. It is all through the love of God, and belief in His Son, Jesus and in Jesus's resurrection. It's as simple as that to start. Then, it's learning more and more about Him, how to be like Him, how to obey and follow Him, how to tell others about Him"

"If being a Christian makes a man behave as you do, then I want to be one. But can I, a slave and a harlot, be a Christian?"

"Ignatius told me that Jesus once told a woman who had sinned with many men that he forgave her past sins, and that she should go and sin no more. In that way, you, too, can be forgiven, if you repent of your sins. Then Jesus will accept you as His own and you will be a Christian as much as anyone, even as much as Ignatius."

I prayed quietly with Isabella that she might repent and accept Jesus as the Lord of her life.

Standing up from my knees, I went over and sat on the side of my bed.

"Come to me," I said.

She did so eagerly. As she sat down beside me, I said, "Put your hand in my pants pocket."

My army pants lay on the bed. "Reach into my pants pockets," I directed.

Reaching into the deep pockets of my army clothing, she pulled out a good-sized bag that I had prepared especially for her.

"Is this…is this money?" she asked in disbelief.

"Yes."

"Is it for me?"

"You will find that it is enough to buy your freedom. Take it and do that with my blessings and with God's. I love you."

"Oh, my dear. I love you, too, so much."

"Not like that," I laughed. "I can see that it will not be easy for you. You must continue praying and seeking God and surrender all your lusts to His way. You can buy your freedom from whichever man owns you with the gift I gave you, but you will not truly be free unless you accept the gift of Jesus's salvation and let Him free you from the lusts of your flesh."

"Oh, I believe. I believe. But I still love you. God's way and the other way."

"There is only God's way," I laughed. "Maybe someday, in God's time, you will understand. Besides, it would not be a smart thing for any woman to plan a future with me, because mine is too uncertain. Oh, before you go, let me be sure that you told me everything Ignatius said to you. Did you tell me everything—every word?"

"No. I would have, but you cut me off."

"Sorry. I was just overly anxious. But tell me now."

"He said you must be strong in your faith, strong enough to suffer for it as Christ suffered for you. Pray that the Holy Spirit will strengthen you so that you might win and that you might win men to Him. Is that confusing?"

"No. It's not confusing at all."

"Look. We will not visit again. I will tell Macennius that I have had my fill of you and that you now bore me. That is a lie, which as a Christian I should not tell. But I think it is necessary to save your honor and mine. In this I am like the harlot, Rahab, who lied to protect God's spies in a foreign land. Well, forgive me for saying this, but you are a harlot by your own words, and while I am a Roman, I have never before been to Rome, so in that sense Rome is a foreign land to me. Is that too contrived?"

"Yes. I would say it is very contrived," she laughed.

"But could you tell me the story of Rahab?"

As much as I can remember, I will. Ignatius told me about her by way of showing that God uses sinful people, even a sinful persecutor of Christians like me, to serve His good purposes, and to show how He redeems the lost if they acknowledge and choose Him. In other words, it doesn't matter what bad things you've done, nor how bad they are, if you repent—decide to turn around—and to accept and serve Him, God can and will use you to enlarge His work."

Isabella looked at me hard, smiling coyly, and I couldn't tell whether she admired my message or was admiring me.

"Are you listening to me, Isabella?"

"Err, err, yes," she said. "I am, I am. Please continue."

"Not if you focus on me. This is not about me. This is about God and your salvation!" I said, rather salty. But, I got her attention.

"I am, I am listening Aurelius. Please continue. I'm sorry."

"Okay. Anyway, the story is that in the days long before Jesus's time on this Earth, His Father, God Almighty, established a covenant with the nation of Israel, under which, among other things, He promised to give the Israelites a land called Jericho. When they came near the land, their leader, a man named Joshua, sent spies into the land, so that he could devise a plan to conquer it. Now, it somehow became known to the king of the people of Jericho that these spies were in his land and that they may have lodged at a house belonging to Rehab, a prostitute, a harlot.

But when the king's men came searching for the spies at her house and ordered her to bring out the men who were in their country to spy it out, she hid them under the flax of her roof. Then, she went out and told the king's men a big lie—that though the spies had been at her house, they had left in a hurry and that should rush after them if they hoped to catch the spies. "Pursue them quickly," she encouraged the king's men, "for you may overtake them."

"Why did she do that?" Isabella asked, confused.

"Because she had said to the spies previously that she knew that the God of Israel was the true God in the heaven above and in Earth beneath. Therefore, she knew that the Israelites would defeat the king and his men and conquer the land. Believing this, she bargained with the spies that when Jericho fell to the Israelites that the spies would save her and her household from destruction when God gave the Israelites the victory. She was a great woman of faith," I finished, proud that I was able to share Ignatius's teachings about Rahab.

"My goodness!" an excited Isabella exclaimed. "So did…was her whole household saved?

"Yes, it was. That was God's promise to her through His servants. God always keeps his promises. All we have to do is acknowledge His power and sovereignty, believe in Him, turn away from sin and serve Him. That's what Rehab did. And, more than that, because of her faith in the living God, the children of Israel captured the land promised them by God. Isabella," I said, in as measured a way as I knew how to do, God can use you to serve His kingdom, even to save His kingdom, if you choose to let Him."

"Oh, dear Aurelius, I want to have your faith. I want to do great things in my life for your God, for Jesus.

"Then, let us pray together, again. Repeat after me: Dear, God, I am a sinner. I believe that Jesus is the Son of God and that he died for my sins. I am sorry for the wrong things that I have done. Please forgive me. Thank you for your offer of eternal life, and for the abundant life you promised here on Earth. I accept Your offer today, right now, and I believe that I am saved. From this day and for the rest of my life, I will follow you."

And as the Holy Spirit convicted her, Isabella cried out repeatedly, through a flood of tears, "Thank you, Lord. Oh, think You Lord."

I cried tears of joy with her, holding her closely until her our tears ceased falling.

"Are you okay?" I asked.

"More than ever before," she answered.

"Okay, then, now we must get back to the business we started a bit ago. Remember sometimes it may be good to do a little misleading for the good of God's kingdom. Remember, that's how we got into the Rehab story. So, could you go to Macennius and tearfully tell him that I sent you away, having become bored with you? In that way you might reenact, in a sense, the essence of the Rahab story. What do you think of that approach," I asked, smiling coyly.

"I think it would be a lie to say that you are bored with me, either way. And I think it is a lie to say that I am a harlot, because I was never one of my free will. Now, I will never be one again, in my new freedom...and because of you, this lie to Macennius will be the last lie I will ever tell, too."

She looked at me pensively.

"Perhaps, when I am free, I will change my name. Neither my parents nor I chose the name Isabella. I think I will choose the name Rahab. That is an honorable name, no?"

"Yes. Rahab is an honorable name. God the Father made it so."

"Perhaps, when others see that my name has been changed, then, as Ignatius says, I will win them to your faith, our faith, no?"

"Perhaps, but when others see that you have changed to be like Jesus, that is when you will win them for Him. Rehab's name is honorable because of both her faith and her works on which her faith was grounded. God the Father made her name honorable forever, placing her in the genealogy of Jesus, His Son. Though God has given honor to that name, you will not become righteous or good like Him by merely adopting it, nor will you lead others to Him through just adopting her name. Rather, it will be through adopting Jesus and all that he stands for that taking the name Rehab will be honorable for you."

"Thank you. I accept all that you have said."

"Then, yes. You will. I believe that when others see you that you will win them for the faith."

Chapter 15

Killing Anger

"Then said Jesus unto him, Put up again thy sword into his place: for all they that take the sword shall perish with the sword."
—*Matthew 26:52 (KJV)*

"I heard him with my own ears," Antonius. "I was standing with my door open when Macennius and Aurelius were talking in the hall. He, Trajan, is planning to give a tribute to Aurelius. And the effusive praise heaped on this betrayer by the Praetorian Prefect sickened me. I had planned to tell him about Aurelius's infidelity to Rome. But after hearing Trajan's chief bodyguard laud him, how can I possibly approach him and expose Aurelius. Still, we have to stop their plan. We cannot permit the emperor to give tribute to Aurelius. By Jupiter, that can never happen!" Publius stormed.

"Calm down. There are other ways…different avenues. Aurelius said that Trajan will not believe words spoken against him unless he confirms the truth of them. That must be our key," Antonius cautioned.

"But…that can only happen when he stands before Trajan, if he does, and there is no certainty of that from what Macennius said to Aurelius. And, if and when he does, is he to be expected to shout, 'I, your Captain, Aurelius Maximus, am a Christian'? I think not!"

"It must be our job, then, yours and mine, to make sure that he does not appear alone before Trajan, but that we are all there with them to force him to deny our accusations."

"And you believe he will deny them?"

"I cannot tell. I do not know if he is the same man anymore. He has become so mysterious. Yet unless the question is put to him, in that place, in that way, none of us will ever know."

Antonius had a difficult task managing Publius. Thinking him too unpredictable, he decided to bide his time and approach Macennius alone, in the guise of a chance meeting, without the baggage of Publius. So, he watched Macennius's movements and, at an hour that he knew he would pass near his office, he stationed himself there, near his office door, pretending to read.

"Oh, good day, sir," Antonius began. "I'm sure our esteemed captain has already thanked you on our behalf. But may I also say that we deeply appreciate the fine way in which you are boarding us? The accommodations, the food and wine, the touring, all are exquisite."

"Well," Macennius said, clearing his throat in a grunt of disapproval, "he has indeed. But thank you, anyway. What is your name?"

"Antonius, sir. Aurelius picked me for his troop because of my excellence as a spearman. Thankfully, we saw no action on our trip. I think it was because in choosing men of combat reputations, he ensured that none wanted to test us. Thus, the successful completion of our mission. Aurelius did an excellent job, sir."

"Yes, yes, I know. I…we are all justly proud of him, as we are of all of you. Now, I must be on to my duties."

"Yes, sir. But could I trouble you with one last thing? I do not want to speak out of turn, but…"

"Antonius, you already are. Your expressions to me should be made through your captain. See that you do so in the future. But… since you are my guest…go on with this one last thing."

"Yes, sir. It's a sensitive matter, the kind that I could not talk to my captain about. One of my men, though not I, heard that the emperor might receive and recognize him, maybe present him some special tribute. That would be well deserved, of course, but, sir, we so respect our captain that every man in his troop would like to be there, if possible, to add words of commendation, or at least just to witness it when it happens. This has been a memorable journey, and seeing him honored would make it one that, well, as old men, we could tell our grandchildren about."

"Are you patronizing me as an old man?"

"Oh, no, sir! No, sir. Nothing of the kind. You are as fit as…"

"Stop it. I was only having a bit of fun with you. What you say is admirable. I can feel in it the respect you and the others have for your captain. I have noticed over the years that he is an aggressive leader, but that his men esteem him and follow him wherever he leads."

And then he added, with a twinkle in his eye, "And if I may say so, they will follow him to attractive destinations as well, by making a not-too—transparent attempt to get themselves into an audience with the emperor."

Antonius did not know what to say. Then Macennius burst out laughing. Cautiously, Antonius joined him.

"I will see if that can be done. No promises."

"Thank you, sir. I will tell the men. Maybe, but of course it is up to your discretion, I would suggest that it is best to not inform Aurelius about it. It would be a good surprise for him."

"Yes. Yes… Good." And Macennius turned to walk away.

"And, forgive me further, sir…"

"What is it now? Antonius, too many questions and too much talk is bothersome. Ruinous. Once your point is made, leave it. Especially with busy men…" Then, Macennius, thinking that this man loved Aurelius as he did and just could not help himself from wanting to find other ways to honor him, relented.

"You've got a moment. Go on."

"This Ignatius was particularly irksome to Emperor Trajan. Would that we could parade him to the steps of the senate in chains as a show of what happens to Christian fanatics. Again, this doesn't have to involve Aurelius, for Ignatius is your prisoner now. But, though forty-five thousand may witness his execution in the Coliseum, if we paraded him, four hundred thousand might witness his humiliation and glory the gods of our state."

Macennius was puzzled. Why was this Antonius pushing these things so much, these secret things?

"I will reject that idea," he abruptly announced. "It takes away from the purpose of honoring Aurelius, if even that can be done. You may have asked too much and had too many questions." Then he stalked off without another word.

Antonius wanted to kick himself in the groin. He'd had everything right where he wanted it and then he might have gone for too much and turned Macennius against accommodating him...them.

Meeting with Publius a few moments later, Antonius approached him with his head slightly bowed. Antonius sat down heavily in a chair next to him.

"Well, what did he say?" Publius asked.

"He said he might do it...that he would see. I think he will when he thinks it over. It is clear that he wants to do what is best for Aurelius. And our proposal is best..."

"Why this double-speak, Antonius? Did he say yes or no?"

"Well, he turned me no direct answer. I could not press him for a clearer response. I did all that I could."

"Would that I had been at the meeting with him. I begged you to do the meeting with him with the two of us. Now, look at where we are! Nowhere! This was our last chance. I am going to go to him myself and ask for myself. I believe he will listen to me!"

"No! He won't. I already saw how he reacts if we try and pressure him too much. I think that's why he turned down my request to drag Ignatius through the streets of Rome—which was your idea, anyway. We can't risk that. We just have to..."

"Be patient!" Publius interjected loudly. "That's your solution to every problem. Sometimes things have to be pushed. If I'd taken your approach in battle, there is no telling how many I would have lost. I have tried your way for long enough. I have doubted myself. But, no more...not again. No more..." and he walked away angry, mumbling.

Antonius could only wait...wait and hope that Publius did not carry through with his threat to speak to Macennius.

On the morning of the fifth day after the arrival of Ignatius in Rome, Macennius and I headed to the seat of government. Today, he would see Emperor Trajan. He would present his palace guards for Trajan's inspection. And perhaps the emperor would be able to see me, he had said. Of this latter matter, he told me that he could not be sure, for the emperor's schedule was crammed full, with obligations with visiting dignitaries in Rome for his festivities added to his usual responsibilities. These guests were important to Trajan, as they would bear witness to the greatness of Rome to the people of their lands, and, being entertained by its choicest spectacles, would be spirited ambassadors in doing so. I rode just beside Macennius, as he required. Though I protested the need for any tribute, Macennius told me that it was not his decision and that he had to make me available to Trajan, just in case.

"You must come. I will not have the emperor say that I have missed any requirement for him," Macennius told me.

"Sorry, Aurelius, given the busyness of the season, I have already informed Antonius that your entire troop could not be a part of any tribute that might be given to you by Trajan and that they should be left at the barracks."

"Hmm. I didn't know that had been requested," I stuttered.

"Oh, it is of no real moment. They all just wanted to be there to witness any tribute that might be given you, or maybe to say a word in support of your good leadership. I think it was a show of sincere admiration for you, but it would have been just too much on a day like today."

Speechless, I knew that something untoward must be afoot. Certainly, I knew that Antonius would not seek an audience with Trajan to praise or honor me. Thus, I inquired further.

"It is good, then, that none of my men are coming. I mean other than Marius, whom I invited myself. As you say, to have them all there would just be too much."

"No, I did not shut them out completely. I'm not that cold-hearted. I told Antonius that he could come alone in order that he would be positioned to describe to the men, first-hand, what went on in the tribute proceedings, if there be any. But, I forbade him from speaking at the proceeding any words he might have in mind for you."

Relieved, I thanked Macennius profusely. He probably thought I was grateful that he would not have all my men there shouting words of support, that I preferred a more modest setting. He could not know that I rejoiced because I felt I'd just dodged a spear thrown at my heart by one of my men—not there to praise me, but in the tradition of Brutus and his Emperor Caesar, to bury me.

⸻

A few days earlier, Publius had badgered Antonius about the arrangement to see Trajan, when Antonius had explained it to him.

"He simply thinks the emperor will have no interest in hearing from any of us on Aurelius, a man about whom he needs to know nothing further. There is nothing that we can do about that. He has chosen me to accompany him on the ride to the Senate tomorrow morning, witness what happens with Aurelius, if anything, and then come back and bear witness of it to the rest of our troop. And that…"

"He has chosen you? You have only presented yourself for his choosing! You kept me away from Macennius and now I know why—so that you could go to the Senate and be in the presence of Trajan and promote yourself. Had you let me attend the meeting with Macennius along with you, we would both be going. Don't tell me you are not as certain of that as am I! This sorry outcome is all your fault!" Publius declared in his angriest tone. Antonius walked out this time thinking that Publius would physically attack him.

⸻

It pleased me greatly to take my friend, Marius, along with me. Doubtless, I could count on his support, whatever came up, and with Antonius there, albeit under censure, Marius gave me a sense of security.

The Forum of Trajan overflowed with dignitaries—senators, tribunes, magistrates, consuls, foreign leaders, and members of

Roman aristocracy. Macennius explained to me that plebeians were kept away, as too many of them posed a threat to security, and, furthermore, if some beggars showed up, the threat of oppressive pickpockets could be introduced in the crowd, and that would give Rome a bad name.

Marius, and I were glad we'd come into the city. There would be stories to tell, indeed, epic tales of Rome and our day in the sun there, tribute or not. The prospect of a tribute, apart from my humility, made me feel a hollowness because I could not share it with my father. I consoled myself with the thought that I would make time to restore myself with my father when I got back to Syria. I would take a few weeks to go to the Arabian Peninsula and make an impromptu appearance at my father's estate. Surely, my father would open his gates to me. And, seeing me in person, surely my father would embrace me and we would talk. Then, I would tell him all about Rome and what happened here.

As Antonius, Marius and I stood at a place designated by Macennius, and as these thoughts of my father crowded my mind, Macennius's shout startled me.

"Aurelius! Aurelius!" Macennius yelled over the din of the crowd. "Follow me. Good news! Emperor Trajan will see you. He seems in a very good mood, but there isn't much time. We're lucky, as it turns out. The gods are with us!"

The gods, I thought. "The gods," I said aloud dryly to Marius.

"Yes," Marius intoned, "I was thinking the same thing."

Antonius turned away in a show of disgust at our exchange. But, he remained quiet. I trusted he would stay so.

Macennius led us around the edge of the Forum of Trajan, avoiding the crowd, past the column of Trajan, to the entrance of Trajan's Temple, pausing there. In the outer court of the temple sat Emperor Trajan, resplendent in burnt orange and red robes, with a headdress resembling a crown of gold with ruby stones. His throne was gilded with gold and embroidered with spring flowers. His statue stood behind him, ten feet high, dwarfing even the tallest man in the assembly. Priests guarded the inner court, wherein only they and Trajan could enter. A phalanx of Praetorian guardsmen situated on either side of his throne, their gladii ready, scanning all who approached. Crassus was beside Trajan, at his right hand, as always. Macennius explained that Trajan did not usually come to his temple, but the press of the day's events led him there for a convenient tribute to meet with me and a few other special guests, while staying close enough to complete his other, more important business meetings.

"Trajan sees his victories in recent battles that he will celebrate at tomorrow's military festivities as tied to the success of your mission to Rome. That you traveled 1,600 miles with your troop without a challenge, Trajan plans to promote as proving awesomeness of the power of Rome. This promotion is well worth the thirty minutes to mark your safe pilgrimage through hostile Christian territory to deliver Ignatius to his death. Don't be bashful in receiving his tribute, Aurelius, because you are a big part of the success story of Rome that Trajan is selling to the world during these festivities. So, soak it all in with pride," Macennius counseled me.

As I entered the area just in front of Trajan's Temple where Trajan sat on his throne pedestal, I dropped to my knees, honoring my emperor, and, too, figuratively thanking him for the chance to have led his troop and thanking him for the honor of meeting with him. Next to me, on my left, stood Macennius; to my right, slightly behind me, stood Marius; and behind us, erect as statues, were posted at least one hundred members of the Praetorian guard, dressed in their white tunics, glowing in the sunlight, their heads covered with white hoods meant to protect them from the heat but that also added to their intimidating appearance. I looked around for Antonius, but I did not see him. "Where is he and what is he up too," I said to myself and not without some concern.

"Blessings upon you, Aurelius. You have done well. I was right to entrust the important mission to you of delivering this blasphemous criminal to Rome, where he will be appropriately punished and our traditions respected. His punishment will be an example to other fanatics. I am authorizing a large monetary tribute to you that I will have in your hands before you leave Rome. You will stay for the festivities? Why am I asking you? I am emperor. I am therefore commanding you to stay," he laughed with all the others. "Take in all that is Rome while you are here—experience it. Taste it. And sit in a special place in the coliseum and witness the final act in this Ignatius saga in which you have played so great a part. There may be a place for you here in the future, a place of leadership in this guard, not just securing me in Asia Minor." Trajan paused to look over at Macennius. "Macennius," he said, "don't take this as a threat to your office, for I am well satisfied with your service. But we must plan for the future."

Macennius smiled, acknowledging the emperor's playful reassurances.

"I am forever grateful to you, Your Majesty, for honoring me with the assignment to bring Bishop Ignatius to Rome. My simple desire is to continue to serve Rome and you. As always, I am at your pleasure," I answered.

I had no interest in the military festivities, and certainly none in witnessing the execution of Ignatius. I began pondering a plan to worm my way out of it. I wanted to simply turn on my heels and head back to Antioch, monetary tribute or not. I'd seen enough of Rome for now. But I could not say such things to the emperor, so I smiled graciously and went along with his light mood. Perhaps, I thought, I could find a way to work an excuse through Macennius, who had so far proven gullible to my tricks. Anyway, Trajan would hardly miss my absence, were I not there, I thought. He would be too busy reveling with people far more important than I.

The brief ceremony ended, and Trajan granted me my leave. But as I turned to go, a voice familiar to me split the air.

"You must not let him leave in honor, Emperor Trajan, because he is a Christian!"

"Who speaks to me without permission? Did this blasphemous voice come from within the ranks of my guard, Macennius?"

In shock, Macennius ordered his guard, "Separate yourselves. Isolate that speaker among you!"

Now isolated, there in the white tunic dress of the Praetorian guard, bearing the same arms as members of the guard, stood a short, stocky figure. Removing his white hood, Publius revealed himself.

I gasped, for I thought surely this must be the work of Antonius and Publius working together for my ruin.

"Your Excellency, I do not know this man. Seize him! Take him from here and execute him!" Macennius ordered.

"Not yet!" Trajan shouted to Macennius. Trajan's face grew grim.

"How did this man infiltrate my guard, Macennius? Who is he? He was close enough to me to have done me bodily harm and without an oath to protect me. How is this possible?"

The temple area fell deathly silent, and it felt as if it trembled, so powerfully sounded the voice of Trajan.

But Publius kept talking.

"I did not know how else to tell you about Aurelius, but I knew that I must. I am Publius, one of the soldiers who traveled with Aurelius as a part of his troop to bring Ignatius to Rome. But along the way, Aurelius became corrupted by Ignatius and I had to…"

"Silence!" Trajan ordered. "Macennius, answer me. How did this happen?"

"Emperor, I do not know. I inspected and counted my men personally, like always. I personally segregated those who would come here for service today from those who would be left at the barracks. I personally looked upon the face of each man I inspected, and after their inspection, I had them hold in a segregated area, pending my order to move out, as I have always done. This man was not among them."

"Since my prefect cannot tell me how you came to be in my temple, in my guard, before you die, you must tell me how this was accomplished!"

"It was not as hard as you might think, dear Emperor," Publius in his derangement, said proudly. "I have been schooled in infiltration by the best, having gone disguised behind enemy lines many times. I simply waited until the inspection ended and the men were milling around, waiting to leave. A few days earlier, I observed that there was one man in the guard of a height and build similar to mine, and I took pains to establish a good relationship with him. After Macennius left, I beckoned for him and he reluctantly came over to see what I wanted. I told him, urgently, that just outside the gate where he stood was one of my troop in sore distress for whom I needed his assistance. As he stepped out of the gate, I acted as if I would show him where my friend lay, leading him from the gate. Thereafter I set upon him and, being stronger, subdued him without his having the opportunity to call out. I then dragged him into a vacant room that I had the night before prepared for that purpose, tied and muzzled him securely, took his uniform and weapons, and joined with his guard as if I were he."

Stunned, the emperor sat looking at this fool of a braggart.

"I did not kill him, Emperor. He is alive and I'm sure ready to resume his service for you. I didn't have any other way to get before you to warn you about Aurelius. Please forgive me if I have done anything wrong, but everything I have done was for the honor of Rome and of you, Emperor."

"You honored neither Rome nor me by your actions. You assaulted, then impersonated, a member of my Praetorian guard. You stole your way into my temple and my presence. You paraded in here and interrupted a sacred proceeding..."

"Oh, no, dear Emperor. You must hear me out. There is one more thing so that you may understand. As it was hot, Macennius permitted the guardsmen to cover their heads. When I found this out in talking to my contact, that's when I knew my plan would succeed. That's why no guard member recognized that I was not one of them, and why Macennius did not either. That is my skill...which I have and can use successfully to better protect my emperor and why I should have been given more responsibility to secure you in Syria, instead of Aurelius. I am completely devoted—"

"You are an insane man," Trajan declared. "There is nothing you can do for this state because you cannot recognize good from evil. You are guilty of despicable crimes. Take him away. Have the lictor behead him! He has made a mockery of my guard!"

"No, Emperor. No! It is Aurelius who should be executed, not me! I say you are a god. He believes in the God of Ignatius. Please ask him and see if he denies Jesus! Please, ask him!"

Publius kicked and screamed at the guard, cursing them coarsely, and cursing Aurelius, and yelling repeatedly, "Ask him! Ask him!"

The crowd shouted him down and laughed at him.

"Do not delay my orders further to send this man to the executioner," Trajan said. "Unless you take him now, all of you who stand near him will suffer the same fate to which he is assigned. And shut him up!"

At that, several members of the guard began clubbing Publius. He fought them off furiously, snapping the neck of one of his tormentors and breaking limbs and face bones of several others. Finally, succumbing to their blows, Publius howled in pain until he fell unconscious. Then, he was dragged, limp, to his ultimate end.

Trajan looked icily at Macennius.

"Macennius, you have failed me. You have put at risk the lives of your men and my own life. You have let the honor of my guard become stained, as bungling and incompetent, unable to police even their own ranks. Your punishment is already known to you. I expect you to carry it out, personally, courageously, without the assistance of any man, within the hour. In that way you may regain some of your honor and my guard's integrity. You are dismissed from my service and my presence!"

———◆———

Macennius's shoulders sagged under the weight of his condemnation. He had anticipated it coming, for he lived with the knowledge of the penalty of failing Trajan. "Forgive me, Lord Emperor. Forgive me," he mumbled. "Forgive me, my men, for bringing discredit upon your heads."

Trajan didn't acknowledge his mutterings. He'd given forty-five years in service to the Roman army, nearly twenty as Trajan's bodyguard and then more than fifteen as his prefect. He'd forgone retirement, at Trajan's request, the emperor contending that he trusted no other man to secure him. And now, not even a look of pity from Trajan.

Macennius thought of Claudius. In this moment, he envied him. He would never see his sons again. They served in the army in posts outside of Rome, and he had only some last few moments to say good-bye to his wife. His family, once revered, now all disgraced because he no longer had a name in which they could take pride. *Better me than my sons,* he offered as a good thought. *I am glad they are away and not members of the guard, as they had wished, for he may have condemned them with me.*

And having considered that, he reconsidered his previous, brief envy of Claudius. Aurelius's fate hung precariously, and he would never know how tonight ended for him. But given Trajan's changed mood and the charge for which Aurelius would be made to answer, with the knowledge that his sons would surely live past this night, he felt himself gaining a morbid advantage over Claudius. He kept searching to see advantage in something for himself this day, even if it involved bizarre reasoning. He went home and kissed his wife good day, forever. Then, within the hour, he went to his barracks, removed his gladius from its scabbard, and fell on it.

———————◆———————

Trajan now turned his attention to me. In an incredulous voice, and with a dry smile, he began gently questioning me.

"Aurelius, what is this insanity coming from the mouth of this fool, Publius? If he had made that charge to me in private, I would have ignored it, but, since he made it in public, I now ask you to answer it to clear your name," Trajan said with a hint of humor.

I looked down. I hesitated Then I heard Trajan's voice, continuing to encourage me to give the right answer.

"You have been like a son to me, and your father, like a brother. But the whole company here anticipates your clear denial of the accusations. No man is bigger than Rome. No Roman soldier, as an officer of the state, may believe in any gods save those of Rome. This, I am sure, you know and understand. If the accusations are true, then you may no longer serve in the army. That much is established as an absolute rule. Do you deny Publius's charges?"

I felt tortured, and must have looked that way to Trajan too. An almost frightened look darkened his face. I'm sure his heart bled for me.

"I will rejoice in my heart with you, and have you stay in Rome. I trust you to guard my life more than any man. Deny the wild charges of that mad man, Publius, and, if you do," Trajan said in an almost pleading voice, "if you do, if you deny his charges, you will stay here in Rome with me, becoming my Praetorian Prefect in place of Macennius."

My heart was immediately torn. Since I had been appointed to command the security forces in Central Asia Minor, for the major forts there and for Trajan and his dignitaries when they traveled and visited there, my father had hoped and dreamed that it would be a path leading to Rome and the dream position, Praetorian prefect. I had supposed that the odds of that happening were bewilderingly long, and that if it came within reach at all, it would be many years removed from today. And, even then, I would have expected a stiff competitive contest of some sort for it. Now, it had been offered without a fight, in fact laid in my lap. I just had to pick it up and embrace it and it would be mine—and mine now, this day! I thought again of my father—how proud and fulfilled he would be, forgiving all, for certain. I knew that my father wished nothing greater for his son than to serve Trajan at the highest level, and I knew that Trajan wanted it for me, too. Trajan loved my father, I knew, and he was giving every indication today that he loved me as well—and even, perhaps, that he had made the offer to me that he'd made with his close friendship with my father in mind.

Time seemed to stand still. Then, I did what Ignatius taught me to do whenever he needed to know what was right. "Pray and ask the Holy Spirit to guide you," I heard Ignatius whisper. Then, as clearly as I had heard Trajan's voice speaking to me, I heard the voice of the Holy Spirit:

"For what does it profit a man, if he gains the whole world and loses his own soul?"

And then an intense feeling grew inside of me, crescendoing in my crying out, words bursting forth that I could not control, "I CANNOT DENY HIM!"

I saw Trajan look over the shocked faces of his guard, and his audience, many with their mouths agape, trying not to utter sounds that might annoy or enrage Trajan. No one dared say a word. I stood frozen.

Trajan called Crassus to his side. I stood close enough to hear him whisper to Crassus: "*This fool, Publius, was right. But, why did I force the question so openly. I guess because it seemed beyond belief that he would answer as he did. I should have declared this meeting adjourned and attended to this matter privately. Now, he speaks, seemingly not in his own voice, but as a man possessed. Oh, would that this day had never come, this most miserable of days. To lose Macennius, my faithful servant and friend, and to lose Aurelius, like my son, and forever the friendship of his father, my brother, is hardly possible to bear. Perhaps, if I had given more thought this time without speaking, I may have happened upon a way out of this quandary.*"

Crassus, seeing and hearing the near unarrestable hurt threatening to swallow his emperor, decided to intervene. "Your excellency, you cannot look weak and indecisive, and no matter what you must do with Aurelius. It is unacceptable for you to be thought either of those two things."

Trajan nodded agreement and I continued quiet, praying silently for guidance, praying against fear and for courage. Then, I heard the voice of the Lord, in the same words that Ignatius told me that He spoke to Joshua: "Be strong and of good courage; do not be afraid, nor be dismayed; for the Lord your God is with you, wherever you go." A peace came over me. The unmistakable peace that only Jesus provides.

I hardly heard Crassus ask Emperor Trajan aloud:

"May I inquire, sir?"

"Yes, Crassus. Please," Trajan answered resignedly.

"Do you love Emperor Trajan?"

"I do. With all my heart. I would gladly give my life in his service or defense."

Trajan's heart, appeared to gladden for he started to feel that Crassus might guide him out of his dilemma.

"Against all enemies?"

"Yes. Absolutely. Against all enemies."

"Against Ignatius?"

"Yes. It is my oath to protect Emperor Trajan against any man who would come against him."

"Good, Aurelius. Then, against Jesus Christ?"

"You have asked a confusing question, Crassus, for Jesus Christ is neither a man nor an enemy of Emperor Trajan, nor could he ever be. He loves Emperor Trajan, as he does all men."

Now, the crowd could not help exhaling, and loud gasps rumbled across the audience.

Depressed, Trajan lowered his eyes and his expectations for Aurelius's rescue.

"But, Aurelius, think well. Though it may be your conviction that Jesus is not an enemy of our emperor, allow for the hypothetical possibility that if he turned out to be opposed to him, in that hypothetical case, you would not possibly take the side of Christ over your emperor, would you?"

I prayed quietly, again. And, again I felt a prompting that rushed convicted words from my lips: "JESUS CHRIST IS LOVE. YOUR HYPOTHETICAL IS FALSE. IT IS FALSE!"

With my voice again rising, both Crassus and Trajan had to realize that the cause of saving me, for which they had both fought, was a lost one. Seeing that I was probably completely unsalvageable, Trajan nodded to Crassus to put the two, ultimate, life-and-death-defining questions to me.

"Aurelius, do you believe that Jesus Christ is the Son of God, resurrected from death after being crucified by Pontus Pilate, and that he is the Messiah, come to save the world and establish a new kingdom?"

Determined not to debate further, and filled with the Holy Spirit, I answered resolutely, "I do, proudly."

"And do you believe that this Jesus is equal to Yahweh, that they are one, and that together they are gods superior to Trajan and the gods of Rome?"

Without hesitation I again answered, "Yes. I do. I absolutely do. I honor Emperor Trajan as my emperor. But there is but one true and living God and He is Yahweh and his Son, Jesus, Incarnate!"

The crowd groaned and, becoming unleashed, called out, "Kill him; execute the traitor; send for a lictor. Blasphemy in the Trajan's Temple demands nothing less."

"Execute him, now," they chanted repeatedly, "Execute him! Behead him! As the chorus rained down calls for my execution, I looked at Trajan and knew that all of his love and kindness toward me had gone out of him turning him now fiercely angry and intolerably embarrassed.

"How could you dishonor me in this way before my men and my friends, before all Rome? You leave me no choice. You have proven yourself useless as a soldier and a friend. Even Claudius, your father, in my position, could not permit you to live. Crassus ask him the one final, final question. Let's get this over with. You know what it."

"Aurelius. Aurelius. Hear me. Will you recant your profession of faith in Jesus Christ and live? Will you take back your words that you may live in the land of your father and with him in his old age, or will you further disgrace him and Emperor Trajan, your friend? "Crassus intoned, almost as a final plea to me to save myself.

But these were the words of my dream. The picture in my vision, where I became one of them, and Trajan asked me to renounce Jesus. It was not Trajan asking the question, as I saw then, but Crassus. Yet, since Crassus spoke with the voice of Trajan, the voice was the same. My dream, which changed from a nightmare to a beautiful hope, was now an unbelievably wonderous reality.

"No, My Lord Crassus, I cannot," I responded respectfully. "With great love for my emperor, but greater love for Jesus, I will not recant my words. I will not renounce Him."

"You have placed the gods of Rome under relentless attack Aurelius, then so have you attacked Rome. You are not bigger than Rome." Crassus now shouted in disgust.

"Your own words have convicted and condemned you. Therefore, on the same day, in the same hour, that the traitor Ignatius is to be executed by the teeth of my lions, you will suffer an equal fate. Take him away to be held to be executed in the coliseum tomorrow," Trajan added in a loud voice, seeking to sound even more set in his purpose than had I. His tone now was unfeeling, as it had been with Macennius. It dripped in revulsion.

I placed my hands before him in surrender, as Jesus had surrendered in Gethsemane. As I was led away, I searched the crowd for the face of my friend, Marius, but I did not see him.

———•———

As the confrontation between Aurelius and Trajan grew dark, Marius had stepped back into the crowd and hidden there. Now, he stood weeping as the soldiers took Aurelius away. He was a Christian, he told himself. If asked the same questions as Aurelius, he would have given the same responses, he tried to make himself believe. The same was true for all of Aurelius's other men who had converted to Christianity—Otho, Decimus, and Valerius—he kept saying in his and their defense. In fact, he was a Christian, but yet a babe in the faith. He did not speak up for his friend, did not volunteer to support him, did not profess his faith, but concealed it. He did not really know for certain what the others of Aurelius's troop would have done, those who, like him, had studied at the feet of Ignatius, he just told himself encouraging things so as not to have to cope with his failure. Even as he thought these things, he continued slinking back into the crowd, finally slipping out and running away.

Marius saw Antonius notice him slinking and whimpering and feared that he might bring him to the attention of Crassus and the guardsmen to force his confession. He didn't know that he needn't have feared that for Antonius didn't know Crassus or any member of the guard, and, besides, Publius had not included him in his plot. Indeed, Antonius's only connection to the proceedings in Trajan's Temple was through Macennius, now banished to a terrible place. Realizing this, he let Marius go. Besides, if Marius could have, he would have realized that the weak-kneed Antonius had seen more bloodshed than he could handle, including that of his friend Publius.

Yes, Antonius and Publius had prevented Aurelius's tribute. But was it worth the price? The plan that Antonius and Publius would gain the Emperor's favor and live in luxury in Rome had been lost as surely as had Aurelius's prize. Certainly, it was not worth it for Publius, who had paid the ultimate price. Publius had raised his angry sword for the last time and it had killed him.

All would not be lost for Marius. He would later tell the men of all that had happened in Trajan's Temple that day, of Aurelius's courage and sacrifice, and the faith of all of them would be strengthened. They would become ambassadors for Christ.

CHAPTER 16
JUST DESERTS

"Fire came down from God out of heaven, and devoured them."
—Revelations 20:9 (KJV)

Rome was bloodthirsty this March, perhaps a curse revisited from the time of Julius Caesar. The already-shed blood of Publius and Macennius amounted to drops in the bucket of Rome's insatiable blood appetite. The city would soon mix their blood with that of hundreds of animals to be sacrificed in temples and arenas, of slaves and gladiators, and of Ignatius and Aurelius, the last two, in the cruelest of all—Rome's sport of Imperial punishment.

The real-life, unfolding tragedies, the killing of Ignatius and Aurelius, other Christians, and random slaves, would play out on the figurative stage of the grass and sand of the Roman Coliseum. The acts featuring Ignatius and Aurelius would be the finale for the cruel crowd of forty-five thousand or so in attendance. The opening/warm-up acts involved men and beasts—slaves fighting lions and leopards, to the deaths of either or all. Brisk betting took place on how many slaves would die before the lions or leopards were destroyed. Betting on the probable winners of the next set of acts—slaves versus gladiators and gladiator versus gladiator death battles followed. A pause to clean up the mess of blood and gore, and then a glorious parade of smartly dressed-out soldiers, powerful horses, and puffed up dignitaries in magnificent chariots, including Trajan, in the gaudiest chariot of all. Towed by slaves or horses, perhaps with scores of recently captured slaves going before them, this parade preceded the last, the final act.

The dessert for the hungry assemblage. The laughing matter. The matter drawing the loudest cheers and jeers. The gross destruction of Christians, fools to be mocked in the eyes of every civilized attendee, by the terror-inducing roars, the fierce looks, the iron claws, and the ivory-hard teeth of huge African lions. Trajan destined Ignatius and Aurelius the tragic stars of stars in this finale, for after the deaths of lesser Christians in this drama turned comedy, Ignatius and Aurelius became the gross laughingstocks for the multitudes, the last and most lasting memories for them of today's events. Yes, March would be gone tomorrow, but if Rome had its way, it would not pass without its blood lusts being fully indulged and sated. Yet, when blood starts to flow, it seeks its own spaces, and can turn in unexpected directions and spurt out from new and unanticipated sources. Thus, it would be on the day next coming.

Tonight, though, Ignatius stared through the dimness at Aurelius in his holding cell in the dungeon, situated next to his own. Fifty yards away in the barracks of the Praetorian guard, Aurelius, just the night before, had enjoyed the most elegant rooms and kingly treatment he could have desired. Now he stood a prisoner, less than a slave, and more than that, a condemned prisoner, the worst estate of all prisoners. The numerous lanterns in those barracks kept the slaves busy re-lighting them, but the dungeon cells let in only the slightest moonlight, through a tiny window, just above ground level, for the dungeon cells were below ground. Enough light got through, however, for Ignatius to see the effect of the horrible beating that Aurelius had suffered at the fists and clubs of the Praetorian guardsmen.

"You would lead us, you scoundrel, you deceiver, atheist!" they had cursed him as they wailed away at him. "You dog," they scolded and berated him, beating him for the sake of the office Trajan had offered him, over them, just hours earlier. Their anger might not have been directed at Aurelius because of his denial of Rome's gods only. It might also have been because of the overall sour feelings that possessed them over the loss of Macennius, whom they revered.

"If you had not brought that impudent Publius among us, Macennius would not have been lost, nor would our comrade, Gaius."

Gaius, too, had been sentenced to die for leaving his post.

"If we did not have to save you for the lions, alive, it would be our good pleasure to tear you limb from limb ourselves," one of the palace guards shouted in condemnation.

Such had been the suffering heaped upon Aurelius from the hour in mid-day until sundown on the day that Trajan sentenced him to die in the coliseum. After that, then, thrown bleeding and unconscious into a cold, filthy dungeon cell, he'd found a little relief from the consciousness of his pain in sleep. Now, awakening, his body ached in every place he still had feeling. He raised his hand to his head and felt patches of semi-dried blood. His right wrist was swollen, broken from his attempts to ward off blows. He had been stripped of his uniform and lay naked on the icy stone floor. A grubby tunic rested nearby on the floor, apparently for him. He reached for it, grabbed it, and covered his nakedness.

"Aurelius. Can you hear me?" Ignatius called gently, a little above a whisper.

"I hear you," Aurelius answered groggily. "I can't see you, but I know it is you, Bishop Ignatius. I thought those guards would beat me to death and cheat the lions. But I took their blows without giving in. They could not break me. Now, I am here with you and you may finally know what it feels like to be in the presence of a condemned man," he said, attempting a smile through his swollen lips and a broken front tooth.

"Oh, Aurelius," Ignatius chuckled. "You are indeed inscrutable. I will not ask what befell you. I believe I already know. You could have fallen into this pit with me for one reason only. But do not think of yourself as condemned. Only Jesus can do that, and at this hour, more than any in your life, Jesus delights in you."

"I could not deny Him. I did not want to, but, if I had, my spirit, His Spirit, guided me otherwise. It was as if nothing else mattered."

"Nothing else did, Aurelius. Nothing in this world did."

"Everything is so abrupt. So many things unsettled, with my men, my friends, my father, my post in Syria. I fear what will happen to all who depend on me—who love me. I have made no preparation to separate from them. I do not fear death in this life, for I expect a new life. But I cannot tell you that I do not fear facing lions before I die. I hear they are the most fearsome of beasts."

"God will provide for and strengthen all about whom you worry, in His time and in His own way. As for the lions, you are a leopard, now God's leopard. Remember Publius's words, what he said about the lions and leopards he encountered in Lebanon and Africa—that leopards were more feared and more dangerous than lions?"

"They will not fear this poor leopard in battered human skin. I will pray not to show fear."

"Then, pray, but accept it as God's will for His glory. It will pass quickly…then on to life in eternity for us. Remember the lesson I taught you about Jairus the Jew when his daughter died before Jesus reached her and he thought that all was lost. Remember what Jesus said? Remember?"

"No. I cannot remember. My head spins and aches."

"Jesus said to Jairus, and now I say to you, 'Don't be afraid. Only believe.'"

I was silent for a moment. I tried to lift himself, but cried out in pain, for I found my right ankle broken. Tears, glistened my cheeks in the small glow of moonlight streaming in. I moaned, "I believe, Ignatius. I believe."

Ignatius swallowed a tear.

"Who betrayed you?"

"Publius."

"I suspected so."

"But his betrayal was not rewarded."

"No. Quite the contrary. He died a horrible death."

"I suspected he would miss the reward he sought. Evil thoughts motivated him."

A space of silence again. My heart began to feel troubled. I sought a word of comfort.

"Bishop Ignatius," I began quietly, "Tell me about heaven again."

Ignatius closed his eyes tried and I saw him bite his lips, and turning away from me, tried to fight back his own tears.

Though I believed and trusted in my hope for an eternal life, at this dark hour, I sought the reassuring words of my friend, Ignatius, to strengthen my faith and make me worthier of what lay ahead in the Roman Coliseum and of what would happen after that Coliseum experience.

"Ahem," I heard Ignatius say, and I knew he had composed himself.

"Holy Spirit," my guide and my comforter, please direct my words. Amen." Then, Ignatius began, cheerily.

"Heaven is glorious beyond description, and we will require heavenly transformation to comprehend its glory. Indeed, Scripture teaches that, the 'eye has not seen, nor the ear heard, nor has entered into the heart of man, the things which God has prepared for those who love Him,' so I can only tell you in small part.

But John, in his vision of heaven, said that its brilliance is like that of a precious jewel, like jasper, clear as crystal. The great streets of the heavenly city are pure gold, like transparent glass. Nothing impure will enter them.

The Father, God, is there on His throne, and His Son, Jesus, is seated at His right hand to receive us into His kingdom, where we will be richly welcomed. Then we will be one with Him, as He is one with the Father. We will see Him face-to-face and we will be like Him, transformed into His glorified likeness. Our names are already written in the Book of Life there, which Jesus holds, and we may eat of the Tree of Life alongside crystal rivers. Hosts of angels will sing continually around His throne, melodies too beautiful for our imaginations to grasp. Departed saints are there—Abraham, Moses, Paul, Peter—whom we will meet and know, and together with them, we shall continuously give honor and praise to God. There will be no death, no wars, no more suffering. There will be no hunger, no thirst, no scorching heat, and no more bitter cold. No evil men. No kings.

No emperors. No slaves. No masters. Living fountains of water will spring there, and every tear and every fear will be wiped away.

In this new place that Jesus has prepared for us are mansions set aside for each of us to dwell in with Him. And we will be new, perfect creatures, with new bodies and new lives. Indeed, all things will be new and perfect. Those whom we have known in this life, who died believing in Jesus Christ, we will see and know again."

"I know now why Jesus told Paul that he must suffer for Him," I shouted out, as the revelation suddenly hit me. "In this moment of my weakness, and even more, when the hour of my ultimate suffering comes, I will be made strong through my unwavering confidence in Him and His promises." To suffer like Him for the cause of the salvation of men, is to be like Him.

"Truly, it is as you say," Ignatius declared, proud of the learning of his most precious student. "That is the essential lesson if we live or if we die in Christ. For as our St. Peter, the first bishop of our church in Antioch, taught in his espistle from Rome, encouraging the Christins pilgrims in Asia to be strong as they encountered persecution—we suffer for the glory of God."

"Beloved," St. Peter sweetly said, in that epistle, Ignatius closed his eyes remembering, "do not think it strange concerning the fiery trial, which is to try you, as though some strange thing happened to you; but, rejoice to the extent that you partake of Christ's sufferings, that when His Glory is revealed, you may also be glad with exceeding joy. If you are reproached for the name of Christ, blessed are you."

"Amen, amen," I sighed in peaceful satisfaction.

Ignatius and I quieted, as no further words could advantage us more, our having come to a place where all we could do was to praise and thank Him softly, in our own personal way.

Momentarily, a chilling thought broke my meditation.

Then, I spoke with alarm.

"My father," I cried, tearfully, softly. "Oh, my father," and my tears streamed down.

"He need not be lost, Aurelius. I will pray that he will witness your example and find Jesus for himself."

"Then, pray for him, Ignatius, that he may believe."

"I will, and I bid you to do the same. You have as much right, as God's child, to ask what you will of Him as do I. Ask what you will of Him!"

———————•———————

Isabella hearing the news of the plights of Macennius and Aurelius, became terribly torn. Witnessing the soldiers carrying the body of Macennius form the barracks, and seeing their anger and sorrow, she initially feared any association with Aurelius and Ignatius. But, with a little time to reflect on her love for the two of them, her distress over their suffering and condemnation compelled her to seek them out—perhaps to comfort them in some way; perhaps just to see them for the last time. She decided to risk going to Ignatius's cell, hoping Aurelius would be close by there. As she approached their cells, hiding from the guards in the darkness, she heard their conversation about heaven, felt the heavenly peace falling upon them, and her tears flowed uncontrollably. Finally, she summoned the courage to emerge from the darkness.

"Aurelius! Aurelius!" she said urgently, but as softly as she could.

As he turned toward her, she gasped.

"Oh, Aurelius. What have they done to you? And Macennius? How cruel. I am so sorry. I was so afraid, but I had to see you. Oh, Bishop Ignatius, that was wonderful, what you said about heaven…I believe. Oh, I believe. I want to go with you. Let me go with you."

"Isabella. I'm so happy to see you", I managed to mutter, excitement leaping in my heart. "But please, don't pity me. I will be with Jesus tomorrow in the glorious place of which you just heard. Oh, I wondered if I would see you before tomorrow. God answered my prayer. Now, you must be careful. Go back to safety from these scoundrels. God still has work for you to do on this side of heaven. So get busy doing it. Heaven will be waiting for you in due time."

Then, to amuse her before she left, I asked her playfully, "So, tell me. Is it still Isabella?"

She smiled.

"No, of course not. I told you I would change it and I did. It's Rahab. Call me Rahab. I will make it official in a few days when I buy my freedom."

Then, she touched her hand to mine through the bars, and I felt her warmth and love.

"I will always think of you, Aurelius, always, with love."

"Rahab," Ignatius said wistfully. "A lovely name. Just lovely."

"Rahab, you must go now. But I want you to promise me that you will search out my father, Claudius Maximus. Ask after him in Antioch and any there can direct you to his estate. Tell him all that you have seen of me, experienced with me, since my coming here and through tomorrow. Help him to understand and believe. Seek out Marius, my friend, who is still in these barracks. He will help you locate my father. Tell him that I still love him and that I do not fault him. Tell him to forgive himself, and that no one is ever too broken for God to put them back together again. Tell him that I am content, even in this state, and that he must learn the same, wherever he finds himself. Tell him to strengthen his faith so that he may be ready for whatever comes...no... I should say ready to pay the same price that Jesus paid for us. Tell Marius that you saw Ignatius and me in chains for the last time, for tomorrow we will dwell with the Lord in Heaven. Tell him that in heaven, no man can ever be chained. No, tell him, that through belief in Jesus, neither I nor Ignatius nor any man, whether in heaven or on earth, can ever truly wear chains again."

"Anything, Aurelius. Anything for you."

"God bless you, Rahab. I will always remember you, too, with great love. Now, go!"

<hr />

Back at her slave quarters, Isabella could not rest. Though she dreaded the thought of seeing Ignatius and Aurelius killed by lions in Trajan's arena, something drove her to go there, to somehow be with them as they suffered their last on this Earth. She had a rough idea of the way to the coliseum, having been taken there once by Macennius when he needed her to help with a special event. Stealing away from her place, she crept along the wall line of the barracks, past a sentry looking away from her at just the right moment, slipping away in the shadows of the trees around the barrack's property, trees standing as silent guard from enemy assaults. She had never been beyond the barracks grounds alone before. Fear gripped her. She shook at every sound sight around her. A beggar called out to her, and she hurried away, not knowing whether his intentions good or evil. Then, she stopped for a moment, recalling Aurelius voice and his teachings about fearlessness.

"Ignatius says that fear is not of God; that He does not give us the spirit of fear."

Then, she repeated it as she pressed on toward the coliseum: "Fear is not of God; God does not give us the spirit of fear."

"Fear is not of God; God does not give us the spirit of fear."

Over and over, she repeated it until it saturated her mind and spirit, and she could think of fear no longer. The shadows seemed welcoming, and every call out from a beggar, a call for her to move forward, relentlessly toward her mission. It would take her hours to get there, to the coliseum, but, she just kept praying for God's help, she felt the warmth of His peace and the guidance of His tender direction, and her confidence soared.

———•———

Among the African lions Aurelius saw at the dock in Puetoli, two were indeed meant to feed on Ignatius and Aurelius. The two largest and most ferocious looking lions, picked under the order of the new Praetoria Prefect, Cicero, a severely cruel man, intended to ensure the most savage of deaths for Ignatius and Aurelius. Trajan wanted a man to replace Macennius whom none among his guard would dare disobey, whether by stepping out of line or by sneezing without his order. After selecting these giant lions, Cicero ordered them separated from the other lions. He gave directives to torment them to put them in the angriest possible disposition. To insure that these lions would attack viciously, he ordered them starved the day and night before the executions, so that their bellies would be empty and their hunger sharp.

Unbeknownst to Cicero, the lion keeper he assigned and instructed in this duty, Brademus, was either a Christian or a Christian sympathizer. In any case, he was an admirer of Ignatius, because his brother, Thaddeus, had been in Thessalonica when Ignatius preached there. Thaddeus had also been a passenger on the ship from Thessalonica that brought Ignatius to the docks in Puteoli. Meeting his brother at the docks as he came to receive the lions, Thaddeus had told him of the cruelty Ignatius had endured at the hands of the soldiers and other passengers, but of the grace, love, and humility he showed in return. Brademus himself had ridden near Ignatius and observed him as he was paraded into the city in chains. He had been impressed at how serene he looked and how he, a man sentenced to be executed, cheered his passage into Rome like all the others. Thaddeus had thought Ignatius a good man who did not deserve to die in the coliseum, ripped apart by beasts, and that thought haunted Brademus this night.

These thick concerns hung heavy on Brademus's heart as he entered upon his duties tonight, the night before Ignatius's execution. Brademus's duty required that he attend to the beasts and release them from their pens into the coliseum when ordered. He thought of washing his hands of the whole sordid matter, leaving the job to another, but then a small voice moved him to a different course.

"Remember this righteous one," he heard a voice whisper. "He has walked before me in truth and with a loyal heart, doing good."

He fell to his knees, quaking in fear and confusion, but he completely surrendered to this power, whomever and whatever it might be.

"What must I do?" he said humbly, looking to the sky.

Then, in that moment he had his answer.

He could not prevent the lions from killing Ignatius, but he could prevent them from disemboweling and eating him. He knew that a lion would not eat on a full belly, though it might kill on one. Furthermore, he knew that a full lion, not aroused by a recent show of hatred from a man, such as by torment as Cicero had ordered, would be even more docile.

At the time set to feed the two lions designated to feed the next day on Ignatius, Brademus separated them from the others, as Cicero had instructed. But, unlike Cicero had ordered, he took to each of them that evening not just the thirty-four kilograms of oxen meat that these big male lions ate each day but triple that portion for each. The lions gorged themselves until they could only groan and lay on their sides and sleep. Brademus left the meat there overnight, so that if the lions had any morning hunger pangs, they could satisfy them.

The next morning, he found the lions fast asleep on the comfortable straw beds he had dumped into their cages to make sure they felt no torment as they rested. A third of the meat was still there in their pens, untouched. He quickly used a long hook to drag it out, so that his treachery would not be detected.

———•———

Isabella leapt in joy as she saw the outline of the coliseum in the dawn's light.

"Thank you, Lord. Thank you, God. Thank You, Jesus!" she shouted out.

Isabella ran, now, forgetting all around her, pressing through the already assembling crowds, until she neared the gates of the coliseum. There she waited, standing in this uncomfortable place, awaiting the opening of the day's events, men pushing against her, scolding her, for she was the only unaccompanied woman among them.

She thanked God profusely again when the gates finally swung open, and she raced as forward as she could. She had no seat that she could claim, but she intended to get as close to the edge of the coliseum floor and maintain her position until she saw Ignatius and Aurelius. Praying that she could stomach these morbid sights, occupied all her thoughts as events unfolded on the coliseum floor. She held onto the rails in front of her, securing her place and giving her something tangible to cling onto should her constitution weaken at the gruesome show she anticipated.

———•———

Trajan had expected this to be a happy day, but he felt gruff and out of sorts. He'd done what he had to do to Aurelius and Macennius, but neither decision pleased him. He'd looked forward to enjoying Ignatius's execution, even hoping to make a friendly wager with Crassus as to how many times Ignatius would cry out for mercy or in fear before the lions silenced him. Now, he'd have to watch Aurelius die with him. He regretted that he'd arranged Aurelius's execution that way. Aurelius had to die. But he'd never before ordered a Roman soldier to die in the lions' arena. This awful punishment of punishments was reserved for no-account slaves and Christians. He'd let his rage cloud his judgment on this distinction and he was paying a price in discomfort for it. Aurelius torn by lions would take all the joy out of watching Ignatius meet his just fate, and this cast a pall over the military festival and other activities he'd planned for the day.

"This will pass soon enough," Crassus soothed him. "We must keep up appearances. Everyone must look on you and gain strength and join in celebrating. If you cheer, the people will cheer. If you mourn, so will your people."

"I know and I will act as you have suggested, but this day cannot speed by fast enough."

Crassus bowed his agreement. Then, he stretched his arms, widening them to cover the range of his glorious achievements, signaling to Trajan to revel in the magnificence of his coliseum and his adoring subjects, to lift his spirits.

The Roman Colosseum was indeed a wonder to behold. To build it had taken the span of the reign of three emperors, Emperor Vespasian (AD 69–79), and his sons, Titus (AD 79–81), and Domitian (AD 81–96). Emperor Domitian's brutal persecution of Christians and Jews seemed to curse the Colosseum to take up his legacy of cruelty.

Yet even under its blood curse, the Colosseum's grandiosity could not be denied. It measured 617 feet by 512 feet, and its seating capacity of forty-five thousand was easily exceeded on this day of celebration, with attendees cramming into every available aisle or space. The arena floor itself occupied area 289 feet by 180 feet. The outer wall rested on eighty cedar piers connected by barrel vaults made of stone. Two parallel passageways encircled the building. Three stories high, the tall columns on its exterior facing utilized the three patterns of Greek architecture—Doric, Ionic, and Corinthian.

The Colosseum's elaborate network of underground rooms and corridors had the capacity to house hundreds of scenery props and hundreds more still of gladiators and animals, all of which could, and today would, be brought rapidly to its floor by an ingenious system of elevators and counterweights operating from as deep as twenty feet below it.

Taking it all in, Trajan's spirit began to elevate. Feeling the coolness generated by the shade of an elaborate awning under which he sat and the constant breeze from the uninterrupted fanning of his trusted slaves, he reminded himself that, indeed, he was a god. Everything around him spoke to that truth, he assured himself, most prominently did the tongues of thousands, in every direction praising his name. He had done what emperors do, in the case of Macennius and Aurelius, protected his realm and its gods. There was only honor in that.

In his special box seating, then, surrounded by a contingent of the Praetorian guard, now more carefully inspected than ever, Trajan feigned regal enjoyment of all of the entertainment set before him. He whispered to Crassus at the fall of a gladiator here or there, appearing to say, "I called that one correctly." And, when three African fighters lost their lives fighting lions before the remaining two killed them, he cheered for the winners. He left his box to briefly join in a military parade, leading it for a while, then retired to his box, letting the long, boring but necessary parade wind to a merciful conclusion. The appetizers and main courses were done. Now, for the desserts.

Lions set upon scores of screaming, immobile Christians, tied to chains that were attached to stakes. Others allowed to run only so far, soon reached the ends of the lengths of their chains. Those few breaking free, were quickly raced down by these powerful, surprisingly fast creatures. Blood smelled everywhere. This time the crowd cheered for the lions, jeering and cursing the Christians, laughing at every attempted escape and every kill made of an awkwardly falling, terrified Christian.

The emperor had planned special billing for his dessert top-pings, Ignatius and Aurelius. As the stars of Christian show of stars in this finale, they merited their own announcement.

"You have seen Christian traitors fall before our gods today in plenteous numbers. For that we applaud the gods of Rome and the Divine Emperor Trajan. We come now to the most spectacular and necessary event of today, the supreme example of what Rome stands against—the spread of Christian fanaticism by those who believe their self-appointed high Christian positions authorize them to dis-honor our divine emperor and our gods. Christian traitors, beware! Beware of your insolence to the Divine Emperor Caesar Nerva Trajan Augustus, Conqueror of the Germans, Conqueror of the Parthians, Conqueror of the Dacians, Son of Divine Nerva, Chief Priest, Acclaimed Imperator many times over, Father of the Fatherland. All fear him! All hail him! Let every infidel Christian fall before him." The crowd cheered wildly, and Trajan acknowledged their effusive praise.

"Today Emperor Trajan has, for your entertainment and to delight our gods, ordered the execution of a high-ranking Christian infidel, demonstrating that none is greater than is he, none greater than the gods of Rome. His name is Ignatius, calling himself, Bishop Ig—"

The crowd drowned him out with jeers, not hearing the com-pletion of Ignatius's name nor any detail of his insolence, as the announcer had planned. The jeers continued, with shouts to bring him out and to bring out the lions ringing throughout. Finally, with soldiers riding around urging the assembly to tone down, the crowd came back to order.

The announcer continued, "And, Emperor Trajan orders for execution, for your derision, a former soldier of the State of Rome, Aurelius Maximus. He is the worst ilk of traitor in the land, a soldier, turned Christian."

Now, the jeers could not be stilled, going on for more than ten minutes, accompanied by fruit and debris thrown onto the arena floor. This time the soldiers made no attempt to quiet the crowd, showing no irritation, for they felt the same disgust toward Aurelius as those in the audience displayed. A soldier of the Roman Empire—a Christian? This could not be. This required that the grossest example be made of him.

Finally, the people settled down in nervous anticipation, set to start roaring again, as soon as they heard the roaring of the lions. The floor of one corner of the coliseum was then lowered, revealing two large pens. Two huge lions stood up, acknowledging the sunlight. The throngs burst into "Oohs and aahs" and wild cheers at the magnificence of these creatures. Their pens were on low wagons, ready to be pulled by slaves to their destinations in the arena. Then, Ignatius and Aurelius, chained and loaded onto a wagon, were towed to the center of the coliseum. The crowd jeered mercilessly. Dragged out and placed no more than fifty feet from the place of the cages holding the two giant lions, the wagon bearing, Aurelius and Ignatius stopped. The crowd's anticipation of the carnage to come reached a fever pitch. In the center of the Coliseum stood a large tripod, with a thick beam across its apex. To this beam the executioners attached the feet of Ignatius and Aurelius, loosely, so that any modest effort by the lions would pull them down from it. Their heads were hung upside down, with their executioners hoping for the exciting spectacle of the lions ripping off their heads and dragging their headless corpses around the ring. And, to the further delight of the audience, disemboweling them, further ripping them apart, eating them, or whatever else they desired to do to them, to their fill.

"Farewell, my dear Aurelius, but not good-bye. We will see each other on the other side."

"I have no fear that we will not. Thank you for what you did for me and the rest of my men who listened, who heard the Word of God and acted on it."

Ignatius closed his eyes and starting reciting:

"Yea, though I walk through the valley of the shadow of death, I shall fear…"

And I joined him "No evil, for thou art with me…"

"Set the lions free!" the crowd roared. "What is taking so long?" others shouted. The Coliseum was alive with whoops and cheers for the lions. "Take their heads off! Take their heads off!"

Executioners, hurriedly opened the doors to the lions' pens and darted out of harm's way. The crowd roared its approval. The ear-splitting chant, "Take off their heads," intensified.

But instead of charging forward and lunging into the helpless and praying Ignatius and Aurelius, the lions lumbered slowly in their direction. And, coming near upon them and finding them silent and motionless, not appearing to fear them, the big cats seemed confused.

Then, suddenly, as if by some mysterious choreography, each lion struck a mighty blow to the neck and temple of Ignatius and Aurelius, almost like an inquisitive, exploratory hard slap, trying to figure out whether these strange upside-down figures would resist or pose any risk to them. But, not knowing their own strength, their blows were so powerful and sharp that they punctured the heads and broke the necks of Ignatius and Aurelius, killing each instantly.

Then, the lions, instead of ripping their heads off and feeding on them, stuffed from overfeeding on tubs of oxen meat and not having any natural taste for the blood and meat of men, laid down and fell asleep.

"What is this? Prod them! Prod them! Attack! Attack!" the people yelled, first at the slaves to poke them, and then at the lions to spring into action. "Kill them! Kill them! Get us other lions!" some shouted.

The crowd shouted every conceivable complaint and every encouragement, directed at the lions, sleeping like pet hounds in the heat of summer. Slaves were dispatched to rouse the creatures. They approached them cautiously, poking them with spears, waking them and rousing their wraths. But the lions' wrath was not directed at the motionless, lifeless, hanging corpses of Ignatius and Aurelius, but at what now appeared to them to be prey on the run, dangerous prey causing them discomfort—the slaves who had roused them. The lions chased one slave down after the other, killing two of them, to the delight of the crowd, before they themselves fell before the spears of the other slaves.

As the calls went forth to release other lions to polish off the corpses of Ignatius and Aurelius, the Coliseum suddenly began to shake violently, as if caught in an earthquake. People shrieked in fear and fled their seats for their lives, trampling, injuring, and killing some of their number.

Trajan's guard hurriedly surrounded him, hoisting him from his seat and placing him on a litter to race him to safety. And then they saw it: a miracle of lights. Two lights hovered over the Coliseum's now darkened sky. Then, the lights sped, in meteoric descent, toward the bodies of the two departed saints. Striking their bodies, these luminous orbs exploded quietly, bursting like soft Roman candle showers, without sound or noise. And then, when the blast of light disappeared, so did the bodies of Ignatius and Aurelius. In their places, surrounded by the light of the Lord, sat a massive angel on a white horse, holding a giant bow, guarding the spot where they had been.

The people stopped their fleeing and knelt down, some falling down on their faces in total awe. From behind the angel's spread wings, two shimmering white light beings emerged, their faces too bright to distinguish, with angel-like form, and quickly ascended into the clouds. And the angel on the white horse ascended with them.

Trajan's men fell back as dead, stiff and unable to speak. Crassus, Cicero, Trajan, and the few guardsmen, themselves nearly paralyzed in fear, rushed, panic-stricken and frightened, from the Coliseum.

Many in the Coliseum, seeing this miracle as a move of the God of Ignatius, believed that Jesus was Lord.

A panicked Trajan was sped to his palace, where he cloistered himself in his bedroom suite, Crassus at his side, as always. All others were sent away.

"I am a god! A god of Rome! Where are the gods of our state? I call on the gods of Rome to favor me!" Trajan wailed piously, desperately.

Crassus was speechless this time, no reassuring words, no soothing words, no confidence-restoring illustrations coming to mind, given the unexplainable events they had just witnessed.

"He was a sorcerer," Trajan lamented. "It was not the fault of Aurelius. He was caught under the irresistible magic spell of Ignatius. I killed him for nothing. Worse, I've put Ignatius's magic on display for my subjects. Now, unless we have a sorcerer, a wizard, a magician, one who can conger up similar public spectacles, my people, from the nobles to the plebeians, will believe him a god."

"Magic, sorcery, I cannot tell. But I've never seen any such display by any magician in the court of any emperor or king, by any man," Crassus conceded gloomily.

"Are you telling me that even you believe that Ignatius is a god?"

"No. I don't think he is a god, dear Emperor. But he may have the favor of a god of whom we know nothing."

"Search the land! Search the world over. Go beyond the boundaries of our empire—perhaps to China or India, exotic places. Find a soothsayer, a diviner, a prophet, a witch, any being who can explain these things and who can give the power to us to know and to use, to master it! Crassus, do you hear me? This we must do!"

Crassus wanted to agree with Trajan. He doubted that he could find the person with the powers Trajan described. But he could not completely deny him.

"I will search, my Emperor. I will search to the ends of the Earth," he said.

Immediately, Trajan's countenance darkened and his eyes bulged. Shock gripped Crassus. For, unseen to him but seen by Trajan was another angel of the Lord, the Angel of Death. He, too, was dressed in white, less luminous than the first angel, but he held a fearsome sword and rode on a pale horse. Trajan heard him speak these words:

"You have seen and yet you have not believed. You seek to destroy the faith of those who have believed in Him."

Then, at once, a fire came down from heaven and consumed Trajan, leaving him an instant pile of ashes.

Crassus's heart raced. He fell, unable to move for a moment, his eyes staring at Trajan's dull, gray, powdery remains.

Oh, my Emperor," he moaned. "My Emperor is no more. What shall I do? What will I tell the people? What will they say?"

Then Crassus remembered.

He hastily gathered up Trajan's ashes and put them in an urn. Then, he went to the crematory in the belly of the palace. There he made a plan.

CHAPTER 17
TO HIS GLORY

"But the word of God grew and multiplied."
—*Acts 12:24 (KJV)*

Trajan had a history of violent seizures. They did not possess him often, but when they came, he flailed and cried out miserably. In their long association, Crassus had witnessed this occurring only six times, the last five happening when he was alone with Trajan, for he had gained the capacity, through careful observation, to know when a seizure was coming on. When he saw those signs, he would hide Trajan away in his bedroom suite and dismiss all of his servants.

Claudius did this to forever guard against any recurrence of Trajan's courtiers, servants, guardsmen, or slaves seeing him in the gross indignity, as he and Trajan saw it, of a seizure. How could Trajan's soldiers and subjects believe and honor him as an inviolable god and at the same time see him screaming like a mad man, unable to control his own body? The first time his seizures overcame him, two courtiers, a household servant, and several slaves witnessed him in his fits. Crassus ordered them each executed, so as to conceal Trajan's weakness.

Trajan had long held another fear that he had shared with Crassus.

"I do not believe it is fitting for any emperor of Rome, and surely not for me, to be seen sleeping in death as an ordinary man, for I am a god. I will dwell in the underworld with all of the divine of Rome. I want men to see and remember me only in the vigor of my ruling strength. So, Crassus, if you be here when my final hour comes, cremate me quickly. Present my ashes to the people as evidence of my death and explain to them the dignity with which I passed from this world to the next. If I should die on the field of battle, wrap me up swiftly with one or two trusted men and cremate me in isolation. If in the palace, then in the palace crematory."

That is why, recalling these words, Crassus had gathered up and cradled Trajan's ashes to the palace crematory while he thought. By morning, he had come up with and put in motion his final plans to ensure that Trajan was remembered with the honor befitting his status as a god.

"Emperor Trajan is dead!" he announced to a stunned group of Praetorian guardsmen, courtiers, and palace servants. "The events of yesterday stopped his heart and called him to the underworld to band his powers with the gods there, to fight together the god of Ignatius and thereby strengthen Rome. I did as he instructed me in writing," Crassus lied, holding aloft a papyrus that he himself had written words upon.

"He ordered me to have his remains immediately cremated. I have done as he wished. His ashes are in this box of marble. You can see that his emblems of gold, which he always wore on his person, bear the unmistakable marks of white-hot fire.

"His successor, he has already named. You know his plans in that regard, for he designated him through adoption this past year. I have sent messengers to inform him of Trajan's death and his ascension, and likewise I have informed the leaders of the Senate and the military. All will support him as our next emperor.

"At hand now is our duty to attend to the funeral of our beloved emperor. This we will do before the sun sets. Our ceremony will be brief and will take place, appropriately, in Trajan's Temple. The public is not invited, only a few dignitaries, to whom I have sent invitations. May Emperor Trajan rest in peace forever, and forever may he guard and favor Rome from the underworld."

"May Trajan's shadow guard and favor Rome forever," they all chanted in the palace and later at Trajan's Temple, together, in a daze, like zombies.

After the invited dignitaries paid their respects, Crassus took control of Trajan's ashes. He and Trajan had secured, for the purposes at hand, the most splendid and expensive urn he could find in Rome, made by a masterful craftsman. On it were depictions of Trajan, presiding, ruling, leading, winning battles. In one picture on the urn, Trajan sat on a throne, lifted off the earth, seated high and alone, looking more like a god than an emperor, above a sea of subjects below him, jubilantly worshipping him.

Crassus made his way alone from the Temple of Trajan to Trajan's Column, carrying Trajan's ashes. The column towered one hundred feet high over Rome. It was magnificently crafted in lava stones and marble from the Greek Isles and featured an elaborate, spiral marble staircase leading to its top, where marble tabletops rested, surrounded by built-in seats of cedar, marble, and gold. At the foot of the column, Crassus turned and waved to the assembled dignitaries. He then plodded his way up the staircase to the column's top, clasping the urn firmly in his sweaty fat hands—in a final desperate effort to assist and preserve the impression of reality in the false deity of Trajan.

Arriving at the column's highest point, Crassus placed the urn filled with Trajan's ashes there, setting the urn down gingerly on a marble tabletop. But as he released the urn, its sides collapsed immediately, and a gust of wind took Trajan's ashes out to sea.

This time Crassus caught for himself the vision of the angel on a pale horse.

When Crassus did not come back down from Trajan's Column, others went up to its summit and frantically searched for him. They found neither Trajan's ashes nor the body of Crassus. Indeed, no trace of Trajan's ashes or Crassus's remains have ever been found.

◆——●——◆

Ignatius's prayers, teachings, and example proved that those exposed to the truth of Jesus, even the most truculent in their opposition, can change—hardened soldiers, bloodthirsty Romans, masters, and slaves. And that leopards, though incapable of changing their spots in the natural, can certainly do so in the spiritual, through the power of the Holy Spirit, when they submit in obedience, because nothing is too hard for God.

Isabella, later assuming the name Rahab, Marius, and the others of Aurelius troop who converted to Christianity, kept the fire of the Gospel of Jesus burning. They traveled the world, converting other souls to Christ. But, they stopped first at Claudius' retirement home.

After God revealed his mighty hand to the people of the Roman Empire, in significant part through the life and death of Bishop Ignatius and other martyrs for the cause of Jesus Christ, Christianity spread rapidly. Indeed, all things were becoming new. Less than three hundred years after the death and resurrection of Jesus, and less than two hundred years after the martyrdom of Bishop Ignatius, Christianity emerged from the valley of the shadow of death, to which Trajan and other early Roman leaders sought to condemn it, to become the official religion of the State of Rome.

HISTORICAL BACKGROUND

Bishop Ignatius was in fact the third bishop of the church of Antioch of Syria in the early second century and an early Christian martyr. Apart from what can be gleaned about his character and thinking from the six letters he wrote to the churches of Rome, Tralles, Philadelphia, Magnesia, Thessalonica, and Smyrna (and a seventh one not mentioned in this story to Bishop Polycarp of Smyrna), few other historical facts about him are known. The messages of his letters, however, reveal the essence of his life—an unconditionally loving and forgiving spirit; an unshakeable faith in the resurrection of Christ; a zeal for martyrdom for the sake of Jesus; and show him a steadfast fighter for church unity and against false church doctrine and false prophets. The letters also disclose most of the trail of his journey to Rome and to martyrdom—the cities he went through, some of the church leaders he met on the way, and something of the reception he received as he traveled. Church lore holds, though history does not report, that he probably met Jesus in Jerusalem as a small child. He was, for a fact, instructed in church doctrine and the principles of Christianity by John, the disciple of Jesus.

We know from his letter to Bishop Polycarp that, after going through Tarsus and the cities to whose churches Ignatius's wrote letters, Ignatius visited Neapolis and Philippi. Thessalonica is not mentioned as a place through which he traveled, but it was on the Via Egnata and on a sea route to Rome. It would have been an excellent place for the soldiers guarding him to winter, as Thessalonica offered many attractions. Of course, he could have continued traveling the Via Egnata to Dyrrhachium, and taken the Adriatic Sea route to Rome, but our story takes him from Thessalonica through the Aegean and Mediterranean Seas to his final destination. The stops at ports in Corinth and Sicily are not based on historical fact, but are stops that would typically be made by a merchant ship to unload and pick up cargo, and for travelers thereon to change onto one ship from another. The cargo that the story attributes as carried by those ships is usual for the time in which the story is set.

The best historical account is that Ignatius was born around AD 30, with most having him martyred no later than AD 111, instead of AD 117, as in this story, making him closer to eighty-one than to eighty-seven when he died. In this book's fictional account, however, his death is moved to that date to correspond with the actual year of Emperor Trajan's death, which was AD 117. Trajan did sentence Ignatius to die in Rome, to be fed to the lions there. But there is no record of why Trajan sentenced him to death, how that decision was made, or the details of his death in the Roman Coliseum. The events surrounding his death sentence and the execution of his sentence in this story are entirely fictional. Yet, an attempt is made to paint a picture of a glorified body based on the words of Jesus in answer to the Sadducees' questions about marriage in heaven, at Matthew 22:30, where He says: "For in the resurrection they neither marry nor are given in marriage, but are like angels of God in heaven." Furthermore, the Angel of Life and the Angel of Death, the former riding on a white horse and holding a bow, delivering Ignatius and Aurelius, and the latter riding on a pale horse, destroying Trajan and Crassus, are imagined depictions from events in the Book of Revelation involving the similar deeds of such angels after the second coming of Jesus. The death of Trajan is likewise an adaptation from a biblical story, in which Herod was stricken by an angel after accepting accolades as a god, dying a horrible death of being eaten by worms. Trajan's death in the story, by fire coming down from heaven, is reminiscent of the consuming fire God sent to quell the satanic rebellion reported in the Book of Revelation.

Ignatius's letter to the church in Rome tells us that he was chained to ten Roman soldiers, whom he called "Leopards." It is not known why he called the soldiers leopards, except that in so doing he does say that they treated him badly despite the kindness he showed them. The organization and dress attributed to these ten soldiers, as well as to the fathers of Aurelius and Marius, the decorations they received, and wars they might have served in are typical for the time period, however. Nothing informs us of the names of these soldiers, their character, backgrounds, training, or personality, making the soldier characters—Aurelius, Publius, Marius, Antonius, and the rest, as well as their ranks and legion affiliations, all part of the fiction of this story.

The heart of the story imagines that in the presence and in the light of the Holy Spirit living in and through Ignatius and the Christians and Christian leaders encountered by these soldiers, it would have been impossible for them to be unaffected by the Holy Ghost's convicting power.

Rome is described mostly as it was at the time that Ignatius died in its Coliseum (the Bath Callica was actually built a few years after). Indeed, it was then a place where civilized people delighted in the spectacle of human and animal blood sports. It was also a place that then deified its emperors. And it is true that Emperor Trajan was deified, even with a Temple of Trajan, in his lifetime and reigned as emperor from AD 98–117, and that he is regarded by many as the greatest military leader of imperial times.

Trajan's Column, raised in tribute to his military victories, stands in Rome to this day. Furthermore, history records that Trajan's cremated ashes were placed at the top of its spiral staircase, at its highest point, by whom it is not known. But it is a fact of history that his ashes disappeared without a trace.

The horrific treatment of early Christians by some Roman authorities and some Jewish leaders is accurate, as are the innumerable acts of love, faith, courage, selflessness, forgiveness, and sharing these Christians exhibited as they endured it. And, thankfully, it is also true that the message of Jesus Christ has continued to spread, despite ancient and modern-day challenges, both in the current persecution of Christians in spots around the globe and in the vociferous presence of those who still deny that Jesus is the resurrected Son of God and the Way by which men may see God and live with Him in His Eternal Glory.

Though history does not record that Bishop Ignatius ascended to heaven as a "shimmering light being" with "bright angel-like form" after his death in the Roman Coliseum, as told in this story.

However, St. Paul teaches of the Christian mystery, in 1 Corinthians 15:50-52, that "We will not all sleep, but we shall all be changed –in a moment, in the twinkling of an eye."

Thus, we rely on St. Paul's record to support that account in the story, for we know that Ignatius and all believers in Jesus Christ will inherit His promise that our corrupt, earthly bodies will be exchanged for heavenly, incorrupt, immortal ones.

About the Author

William Jennings Jefferson spent five and a half years in federal prison, for convictions ranging from bribery, to honest services, and racketeering violations. In late 2017, a decision of the United States Supreme Court overturned these convictions, miraculously forcing Jefferson's immediate release. While imprisoned, Jefferson, active in the prison church and leading its choir and Sunday school, began studying the trials and triumphs of martyrs of the Early Christian Church, discovering the intriguing, untold story of one such martyr, Bishop Ignatius of Antioch, Syria. Desiring to encourage today's Christians, as well as nonbelievers, faced with critical challenges in life, including challenges of faith and of forgiveness, Jefferson, through the guidance of the Holy Spirit, decided to create this Roman a clef, adapting the real-life story of Ignatius and his struggles, and those of early Christians with evil authorities, into a timely and useful Christian fiction novel of hope for life and for eternity. *Can Leopards Change their Spots?* exemplifies the truth of the proposition that, if the Holy Spirit could change evil men of Ignatius's times, through the power and example of love and forgiveness, and inspire prison convicts of today to follow Christ, He can change the lives and convictions of all of us willing to avail ourselves of His overcoming, redeeming power.

Prior to his convictions and incarceration, Jefferson served eighteen years as a Member of the US House of Representatives, representing the Second Congressional District of Louisiana. Preceding that tenure, Jefferson served in the Louisiana State Senate for ten years, where he received numerous awards for excellent service, including twice being named Legislator of the Year by the Alliance for Good Government. Jefferson is a graduate of Southern University, of

Harvard Law School, and holds a master of laws in Taxation from the Georgetown Law School. He has been married to Dr. Andrea Green Jefferson for forty-eight years, and they are the proud parents of five accomplished daughters—three law professors, a film maker, and a physician—and the grandparents of eight.

Jefferson and his wife are members of the Greater St. Stephen Full Gospel Baptist Church of New Orleans, Louisiana, where Jefferson has served as a member of the Church's Trustee Board, and his wife has served as both Chair of the Bishop Paul S. Morton, Sr. Scholarship Foundation, and as principal of the Paul S. Morton Christian Academy.

Previously, Jefferson authored and self-published two books, in part, carrying religious threads and themes, *Dying Is the Easy Part* and *Daddy's Pelican*.